# ALCHEMICAL
# ACTIVE
# IMAGINATION

## A C. G. JUNG FOUNDATION BOOK

The C. G. Jung Foundation for Analytical Psychology is dedicated to helping men and women to grow in conscious awareness of the psychological realities in themselves and society, find healing and meaning in their lives and greater depth in their relationships, and to live in response to their discovered sense of purpose. It welcomes the public to attend its lectures, seminars, films, symposia, and workshops and offers a wide selection of books for sale through its bookstore. The Foundation also publishes *Quadrant*, a semiannual journal, and books on Analytical Psychology and related subjects. For information about Foundation programs or membership, please write to the C. G. Jung Foundation, 28 East 39th Street, New York, NY 10016.

# Marie-Louise von Franz

# ALCHEMICAL ACTIVE IMAGINATION

## REVISED EDITION

SHAMBHALA
*Boulder*
1997

Shambhala Publications, Inc.
2129 13th Street
Boulder, Colorado 8030
www.shambhala.com

12   11   10   9   8

Printed in the United States of America

Shambhala Publications makes every effort to print on acid-free,
recycled paper.

Shambhala Publications is distributed worldwide by Penguin Random
House, Inc., and its subsidiaries.

Library of Congress Cataloging-in-Publication Data
Franz, Marie-Luise von, 1915–
    Alchemical active imagination/by Marie-Louise von Franz.
  —Rev. ed.
      p.  cm.
   ISBN 978-0-87773-589-2 (pbk.)
    1. Jungian psychology.   2. Alchemy—Psychological aspects.
  3. Dorn, Gerhard, 16th cent.   I. Title.
  BF175.F73   1997                                      97-29220
    150.19'54—dc21                                    CIP

# CONTENTS

# ACKNOWLEDGMENTS

THE TEXT OF THIS BOOK derives from the transcription by Miss Una Thomas of a series of lectures given by Dr. Marie-Louise von Franz at the C. G. Jung Institute, January–February 1969 in Zurich. We are grateful to Ms. Thomas for her faithful preparation of the original version.

I want to thank Dr. Barbara Davies for translating the additions of Ms. Francine Perrot in the French edition. My greatest thanks to Dr. Vivienne Mackrell for editing the text with me and her genial support of this effort. I want to thank Kendra Crossen for her patience.

# 1

※

# ORIGINS OF ALCHEMY

## *Extraverted and Introverted Traditions*

BEFORE I GO INTO THE INTERPRETATION of a specific text I want to give you a short history of alchemy as viewed from the psychological standpoint. The birth of Western alchemy took place about the time of the birth of Christ. There were beginnings in the first century before Christ, but these are difficult to trace. Thus one could say that alchemy began in the first century, with a flourishing period in Greece and the Roman Empire in the second and third centuries, followed by a gradual decline there up to the tenth century. During this last period the main Greek texts were transported and translated into Arabic, and in the seventh and eighth centuries there was another flourishing period in Arabic countries, after which alchemy evolved along with the history of chemistry, following the same course as all physics and mathematics. In about the ninth century A.D. it returned to Christian civilization via the Arabs and the Jews in Spain[1] and Sicily, and from there invaded the Western countries and united with scholastic philosophy, and so developed further. Early chemistry is simply the history of one branch of the natural sciences in general.

Western alchemy, in the narrower sense of the word, had two parents: Greek rational philosophy or, you could say, a nature philosophy (I refer mainly to the pre-Socratic Greek

1

philosophers such as Empedocles and Thales of Milet, and to Heraclitus) on the one hand, and Egyptian technology combined with Mesopotamian astrology on the other. The Greek philosophers—who introduced rational thought into their concept regarding the problems of nature, of matter, space, and time—made very few or no experiments. Their theories are bolstered by certain observations, but it never occurred to them actually to experiment. By contrast, in Egypt there was a highly developed chemical-magical technique, but in general the Egyptians gave it no thought, either philosophical or theoretical. This technique was simply the handing down by certain priestly orders of practical recipes together with magic religious representations but without theoretical reflection. When the two trends of Greek and Egyptian civilization came together, they united in a very fruitful marriage, of which alchemy was their child. You know that from Greek philosophy all the basic concepts still valid in modern physics were created: the concepts of matter and space, the problem of time, if you think of Zeno; the concept of energy, that would be Heraclitus; the concept of the particle, created by Leukippos and Democritus; the concept of affinity of the elements, the idea of the four elements, which prevailed till right up to the sixteenth and seventeenth centuries in Western civilization—all these concepts were created by the different pre-Socratic Greek philosophers.

In Greece it was a switch from a religious-mythological outlook on the existence of the world to, for the first time, a philosophical one, in the sense that the basic concepts were philosophical but still filled with mythological mana, so to speak, and very much associated with what we now would call psychological projections. One of the ideas, namely that the basic elements of the universe are mathematical forms, was created through the Pythagoreans and carried on in a slightly varied form by Plato, and is now again of importance in Heisenberg's theory and in quantum physics. Thus there is a strong line going through Greek philosophy into modern science, even though it never occurred to the Greeks to make practical tests.

In Egypt, chemical techniques had been highly developed, but—and this is very relevant—they were used mostly in a specific realm of Egyptian religious life connected with life after death. To give one example: the Egyptians lived in miserable little clay huts, which naturally have all disappeared. Not one private Egyptian house remains, only the great buildings, the pyramids, temples, and tombs. When Jung one day remarked to a sheikh that it was striking that the Egyptians had no good houses during their lifetime but gave all their energy to building their tombs, the Arab smiled and replied, "Well, why should you be troubled about building a house for the seventy years of your life here? It's more important to build a house for your life in eternity!" For him, it was still quite the natural thing to do. An enormous percentage of an Egyptian's energy was directed to life after death, and his main concern was that the right kinds of rituals be performed so that eternal life after death would be assured in the right way. Egyptian civilization is typically African, not Mediterranean. They believed that through the preservation of the body, of the corpse, the immortality of the soul could be assured in a technical, magical way and that immortality was achieved by transforming the body of the dead person into the cosmic Godhead. On the one side, the Egyptians had a pantheon of many gods, but on the other hand, they believed that there was one cosmic Godhead which was sometimes identified with Atum, or with Nun, or with the god Re in particular form, or in the cosmic Osiris, sometimes also called the Ba-soul of the universe. There are different names according to the different provinces in Egypt, but the basic idea is that over all the many gods of the Egyptian pantheon there rules a kind of cosmic spirit, a god that is an all-pervading spirit of the universe who rules all other gods and can absorb them. The dead person was slowly transformed into that god. He took part in a great mythological process that was, so to speak, a mirror of the whole cosmic situation in which the Egyptian felt himself to live.

Toward the middle of the old Egyptian empire, one god in the Egyptian pantheon, the sun god Re, became more and more dominant. This phenomenon corresponds to a typical development of consciousness. It was the time when writing and recording, the measuring and mapping out of the fields, mathematics, and all such arts flourished. For the first time in the Egyptian empire records were kept. Here there is a coincidence: at the time when the sun god, who is the archetypal principle of consciousness, becomes dominant in a civilization, there is a sudden increase in rational consciousness. But naturally through this also arises a split from which we still suffer: namely, that certain aspects of the psychic life of the individual, certain moods and impulses that do not conform to collective rules, have to be repressed. Thus, everybody who owns land is tempted to move the border stone a bit farther out during the night and then to claim, "Well, look! The stone is here, that's where the demarcation line is." That is the old fight for territory that animals carry on and that we still have in us. So you could say that the natural instinctive regulations of life among human beings, based on impulse, aggression, counteraggression, and then the establishment of a kind of relationship like that of animals living together fighting for their territories—all that came to an end, and with that a lot of individual and instinctive impulsiveness was overruled by fixed regulations of law and order, coinciding with the dominance of the sun god Re.

You could therefore say that part of the primitive individuality of the Egyptian went into the unconscious at that time, and with it went a certain aspect of affect in the feeling life. This aspect of the Egyptian's communal life was concentrated in the archetypal image of the god Osiris. Osiris, in contrast to the ordering, ruling sun god, was the suffering god. He represented the passive, suffering aspect of nature and of the psyche. Histories of religion always depict him as the god of vegetation; however, that does not mean concrete vegetation, but vegetation as a symbol of his being: it is that which does not move, which does not have its own volition, which is the greatest suffering thing on this earth. Osiris represents the underground part of the Egyptian communal life. In the Osiris part of his nature was also hidden the Egyptian's true consciousness of his own individuality, in contrast to the collective ruling principle of consciousness. So the body was associated with Osiris and the idea of the Ba-soul.

In Professor Helmuth Jacobsohn's paper, which appears in English in *Timeless Documents of the Soul*,[2] you will find the famous discussion of the World-Weary Man with his Ba-soul, together with much documentation which tends to prove that the true pre-conscious individuality and individual human consciousness was at that time still projected into the Ba-soul. Normally in Egypt the Ba was either represented by a star or a bird. In Jacobsohn's paper you will read that a man was not aware of his Ba-soul during his lifetime, since as an individual he lived according to Egyptian regulations, even to the extent that during the judgment after death he had to swear to a list of things that he had *not* done. That is the famous negative confession: "I have not stolen, I have not broken the law, I have not sacrificed to the god . . . ," and so on. As Jacobsohn points out, that is clearly a nice list of lies, because they did all these things like everybody else, but the idea of lying like that to the gods after death was considered not a lie but an assertion: "I would not dare to impinge on the collective rule." Because to dare to say, "Yes, I have done this," would imply individuality; it would mean standing up to the fact that one had broken a rule, and that was forbidden. Egyptians were so closely identified with the collective ruling body of morale and ideas that they could not admit their individual sinful impulses even to themselves and to the gods.

Normally, you would meet your Ba-soul only after death and be completely unaware of its existence before. It emerged, so to speak, at death and during the mummification process. But in this specific paper, "The World-Weary Man," there appears a man whose Ba-soul suddenly speaks to him during

his lifetime, at the moment when he is about to commit sui-
cide. This results in a very famous and touching conversation
between the two. Such a meeting with the nucleus of one's
own individuality was believed to take place only after death,
the Ba-soul being immortal and individual, the eternal aspect
of the human being. Becoming one with the Ba-soul meant,
therefore, being deified and becoming one with the oneness of
the universe. The Egyptians believed they could bring this
about in a magical way by preserving the body, and there we
touch upon the link between chemistry and religion, for the
main chemical procedure of mummification consisted in bathing the corpse in a base of sodium bicarbonate. Now, the root
of the Latin word *natrium* (sodium) is n-t-r, meaning "god."
So mummification simply meant bathing the corpse in "god
liquid," god substance, till it was completely soaked in it and
became eternal. The corpses actually did blacken and solidify,
and the blackness of the mummies that one can see in every
museum comes from the natrium, the sodium bicarbonate. By
soaking the corpse in the god-liquid it became eternal and
identical with the cosmic Godhead. When bathing the corpse,
for example, the embalmers say, "O So-and-So [the name],
the primordial flood of Nun [the primordial ocean from which
all the gods originated] is flooding into your coffin. Now you
are completely soaked in Nun, now you become Atum the
cosmic god [Atum is the spirit in Nun, its spiritual aspect].
Now you become one with Nun. Now you are Atum. Now you
rise above all the gods, you absorb them all, you are one with
them, they all serve you."

Every bit of the mummification meant the integration of
a Godhead. The linen bandages in which the mummy was
wrapped represented the goddesses Isis and Nephthys. When
a corpse was thus wrapped in the bandages, it meant he was
wrapped up by the right-hand and left-hand brides or wives
of Osiris. At the moment of death the deceased man is called
Osiris and is identical with the god Osiris. This is why, even
in the famous embalming papyrus in Cairo, which hands down
to us the technical rules for the mummification of the corpse,

he is always spoken to as, "O Osiris/So-and-So, now your bride Isis and now your beloved Nephythys come toward you, they embrace you, they keep and preserve you in their embrace, you rest in their embrace forever and eternity." Then gold is put on the fingernails and one says, "Now the gold which belongs to Horus comes to your fingernails and makes you eternal." The whole body was smeared with oil. (The papyrus is completely technical; it says, for instance, that the body has to be soaked in oil, but when it is turned over on its back, one must be careful that the head does not topple backward.) When the body is smeared with oil there follows a liturgy, "O Osiris/So-and-So, now the oil which comes from Punt, now the myrrh which comes from such-and-such a place, the stuff of Osiris, the stuff of the god Wennofre [a title of Osiris]. Horus comes toward you, they make you eternal in eternity," and so on.

So you see that the Egyptians with their actual chemical procedure made the dead person eternal, turning him into Osiris and also liberating his Ba. Parallel to the Indian representation of the cosmic all-pervading Atman and the individual atman in every person—the cosmic Purusha and the individual purusha—in Egypt, Osiris was the cosmic and individual principle in every person. This transformation was brought forth by the chemical procedures applied in the mummification process. Here you are back in the world of primitive magic. African magic nowadays would still be based on this principle, namely that concrete material things are laden with mana, that they are divine things. What is divine? Materials are divine; therefore, if we use any kind of matter, we use a god, or a Godhead full of mana, and by mixing materials, divine powers are mixed and a divine power is exerted, or we bring forth changes within the realm of the divine powers. All Egyptian techniques were used in that magical and religious spirit. The Egyptians had also taken over from the Sumerians and then the Babylonians a highly developed technique of amalgamating different metals, such as bronze and tin, and this was always done in a religious ceremony. When, for instance, iron ore was melted, it had to be done at a certain time of the month when the Godhead of iron was constellated in a favorable way. There is a beautiful film called *Mandara*, named after a tiny little village in the hillsides of the Congo, which shows how the iron is melted and then turned into spears and weapons by one of the village men. Only one village family has this privilege. The secrets of the art are passed down from father to son, and nobody but specific members of this family have the right to perform this work. They melt the iron with the most primitive means, and then the village "blacksmith" continues with certain rituals. During this time the other members of the village have to keep away, fast, and drum. As far as I could see, no direct sacrifices were made, but in ancient Egypt, in most of such traditions, animals or even embryos or human beings were sacrificed. And again we come to an essential part in the whole alchemical tradition, namely a connection between alchemy and astrology. As I mentioned before, you cannot cast or melt iron without waiting for a favorable day. These days are generally determined by the stars: the melting of iron is done when Mars—the planet that protects or corresponds to the metal—stands in a favorable conjunction. For tin, Jupiter must be in harmony, and for gold, the position of the sun must be right. From the oldest times, each planet has always been associated with a different metal; therefore, for the treatment of these materials to be successful, it is necessary to be aware of the astrological constellations.

There you see the archetypal, archaic roots of a concept that Jung unearthed through his acquaintance with alchemy and that is now the great problem in modern science, namely the idea of synchronicity.[3] There is even an expression in Greek alchemy that you can only translate synchronistically. The famous alchemist Zosimos, on whose visions Jung commented,[4] says that there are ordinary astrological-magical transformations of metals based on superstition, and there are Kairikai transformations of metals. *Kairikai* comes from the word *Kairos*, meaning the magically favorable moment, but not only astrologically. It is more or less the Chinese idea of Tao, which one can only reach by feeling: "Not today, not now, but *now* is the right moment." That is Kairos. And Zosimos in a whole treatise says that alchemy has to do with the Kairikai transformations of metals. That means that one has always to find through meditation the right inner moment for the transformation of a material, and not just regard the astrological constellation in a superstitious way. So there arises the problem of science and the still-unsolved problem of time—time, as you know, being one of the great mysteries with which science has not yet coped. But at that time it was observed by astrological means—that was the most widespread way—and Zosimos, a true mystical introvert, attempted to internalize this concept more into the idea of the Kairos, the right inner moment.

The great opposites of human nature in general, extraversion and introversion,[5] play a tremendous role in the history of alchemy as in the history of all other sciences. The Greek theoreticians of natural philosophy had been more introverted and the Egyptian technologists had been more extraverted, but when the two currents met, a strange switch occurred: the Greeks became interested in concrete material and the Egyptians in its psychological inner aspect. In spite of this development, the inner opposition and the play of their introverted and extraverted attitudes continued.

Therefore, from the very beginning, there were always certain chemical treatises in which more emphasis was put on concrete operations: take that and that in such-and-such quantities; see that the material is clean and mix it in such-and-such a way. Or there were sketches showing how to make a furnace and how to form new glasses, retorts, and vessels. From the sixteenth century on, this tendency prevailed, and up to our days science developed in a unilateral, experimental, and extraverted way. If, for instance, you read Holmyard's *Alchemy*, that's what you will find.[6] He outlines the history of alchemy in an extraverted way, and he will tell you only about that. We can say that in modern times a great turning point occurred in the natural sciences; the extraverted line having been pursued to its limit, its exaggeration led into dead ends, and leading people in modern physics endeavored to look once more for the subjective factor. It began with the discovery that you cannot extrapolate the observer from the experiment, and I think this will inevitably lead to the realization that not only can you not extrapolate the observer, but you cannot extrapolate his or her subjective conditions either. We are just now on the verge of turning to the more introverted approach, which shows a greater awareness of the inner state and of subjective and theoretical presuppositions within the experiment.

The introverted approach was represented from the beginning by such people as Zosimos, and among the Arabs, for instance, by a Shiite mystic of the tenth century named Mohammed ibn Umail, whom we find quoted in Latin texts under the name Senior. He was a sheikh, and "Senior" was simply the translation of that title. These alchemists approached the problem from another angle, presupposing that the mystery they were looking for, the mystery of the structure of the universe, was in themselves, in their own bodies and in that part of their personality which we call the unconscious but where they saw the source of their own material existence.

They thought that instead of taking outer materials you could just as well look inside and get information directly from that mystery because you were one with it. Since the adept was a part of the mystery of cosmic existence, he could just as well watch it directly. What's more, he could ask matter, the mystery of which we all consist, to tell him what it is, to reveal itself to him. Instead of treating it like a dead object to be thrown into a vessel and then cooked in order to see what would come out, one could just as well take a block of iron, for instance, and ask it what it was, what its kind of life was, what it was doing, how it felt when melted. Since all these materials are within you, you can also contact them directly. In that way these alchemists contacted what we would now call the collective unconscious, which to them was also projected into their own bodies. They consulted these powers directly through what they called meditation, and therefore most of these introverted alchemists always stressed the fact that one should not only experiment outwardly but always insert into the opus phases of introversion with prayer and meditation comparable to a kind of yoga. With the help of this meditation the artist sought the right hypothesis, or information, about what he was doing or about the materials he was examining. Or he would, for instance, talk directly to quicksilver or to iron—and if you talk to quicksilver and iron, then naturally the unconscious fills the gap with a personification. This is how Mercury appears to tell the adept what Mercury is about and to inform the artist that the soul of gold will appear in order to reveal who and what the sun god is.

Looking backward historically, we can say that what we see now as two things, and which for the sake of clarity we try to keep apart—namely a difference between what in Jungian terms we call the collective unconscious and what in physics we call matter—were, in alchemy, always one: the psyche. You know that Jung too was convinced that they were one and the same unknown, appearing different to us depending on whether we observe it from without or within. If your approach is extraverted and you observe it from without, you call it matter. If your approach is introverted and you observe it from within, you call it the collective unconscious. This dual trend is seen, for instance, in such book titles as *The Physical and the Mystical Things*, which is a famous old treatise by pseudo-Democritus. By *physika* he means the recipe aspect of chemistry, and by *mystika* he means the theoretical religious-philosophical aspect attained by meditation. This twofold aspect still exists today, for instance in theoretical physics, where there is a dual trend of thought.

For original man and archaic man, all materials were—and you could say they still are—ultimately unknown entities as to their ultimate essence. Therefore in the early Greek treatises they bear names that one simply cannot translate.

For instance, sulphur is called *theion*, which also means divine. Then a material called *arsenikon* is often mentioned. *Arsenikon* simply means male, and in contrast to *theion*, you cannot define in old treatises what material is meant by *arsenikon*; it might be anything. Therefore, the translations of old alchemical treatises simply leave the name *arsenikon* as the male substance, because that word covered any substance which was hot and which was "attacking any other substance." So all acids are male because they corrode, they attack other materials. Silver, on the other hand, is female and passive because it is very easily attacked and corrodes easily. Any hot substance that has a tendency to alter other substances chemically was called *arsenikon*. Today it has taken on only one meaning— arsenic—but that was not the case previously. Every author had some specific substance in mind, although we cannot find out which. There are even sentences that contain the word *theion*, divine, and one just does not know if it should be translated as the divine basic mystery of the universe or as sulphur! That's why you can use practically none of the translations, but have to learn Greek and Latin and retranslate yourself.

Because of the extraverted trend of the history of science, modern historians of chemistry always translated *theion* as sulphur, but there are contexts where this translation is extremely doubtful and where one could just as well render it in its other meaning of the divine mysterious substance, the God-mystery within matter. Man's curiosity, which has led him to experiment with materials, was always based on the idea that indirectly he could find out more about the Godhead or the divine mystery, the ultimate mystery of existence. Just as by looking at a painting or at some craft work and wondering about it, one can figure out quite a lot about its creator, so people always thought that in learning about the mystery of the cosmos and existence they would also get closer to that mysterious force which made it, whatever it was.

This mythological archetypal impulse behind the true investigating urge of scientists still survives in the great scientists of today. The ultimate dynamic impulse to become a physicist is based upon the desire to find out more about how God works. When, during a discussion with Niels Bohr, Einstein suddenly with affect exclaimed, "God does not play dice," he gave himself away. Similarly, after hearing that the principle of parity was no longer completely valid but had been broken, Pauli's first words were, "Then God is left-handed after all." That amounted to the same thing! So you see, scientists are still true alchemists, in a modern version, and their interest in investigating the mystery of matter is still not carried only by material impulses, or opportunism, or academic ambition, as it is with minor minds. The really great and creative scientists have the same motivation as the alchemists: to find out more about that spirit or divine substance or whatever you may call it, which lies behind all existence.

This subjective outlook on their own work was characteristic of the alchemists, or at least of the great alchemists. Even as early as the third century they had great difficulties understanding what was meant in the texts of their fellow members. We are not the only ones having a problem translating *theion* as either "sulphur" or "divine," and *arsenikon* as either "acid" or "a corrosive substance" or "the male dynamic aspect of matter." Alchemists were not able to consult with their colleagues, because they were all lonely experimenters and therefore got themselves very mixed up. They spoke both an "exoteric" language (the ordinary language, pointing toward the physical aspect of the substance and operations) and an "esoteric" (symbolic and mystical) language, and thus got into a Babylonian confusion, which they tried to rectify among themselves, saying: "I really mean that, and So-and-So means that, and So-and-So does not mean that." For instance, Zosimos of Panopolis says that the basic stuff of the universe is the mysterious element "omega." In exoteric, nonmystical language that is the water of the ocean, but in esoteric language it is a tremendous mystery that only a certain Gnostic author, Nikotheos, knew about. Ocean water, according to Thales of Milet, is the origin of the world, the *prima materia*, or basic material of the universe, and its outer chemical, banal aspect is sea water. What it really means, Zosimos says, is a Gnostic religious mystery.

Now we come naturally to the collective conscious religious situation at the time of the birth of alchemy. On the whole, educated people no longer adhered blindly to the primitive Greek religious cults but had a half-religious, half-philosophical outlook, while simple agricultural people had an astrological and magical outlook on things. Then, through the spread of the Roman Empire, there came this phenomenon called syncretism. The Romans had a clever way of assimilating people into their empire—by translating the archetypes. If, for instance, they conquered an Etruscan tribe, or when they later conquered the Celtic tribes, they would find out who the main native gods were and assimilated them to their own gods. As they were all Indo-Germanic, they all had the same pattern. The main male god became Jupiter So-and-So and the great goddess Juno or Hera So-and-So, and if the god of commerce was called Kerunnus, he became Mercurius-Kerunnus. Thus we find temples everywhere in France dedicated to Mercurius-Kerunnus. It was a clever trick to avoid fanatical religious fights and to achieve integration into the Roman Empire. It gradually created a kind of syncretistic religion in which people were accustomed to think indirectly in archetypal terms, in the sense that they believed in a certain higher father god, a great mother goddess, a god of intelligence, and so forth. Naturally the Roman's policy tremendously weakened and ultimately destroyed the people's religious outlook, but for the moment it solved the problem and relativized all religious antagonism that would have arisen.

Under cover of these syncretistic religious interpretations, those who were by temperament more religiously oriented generally looked for something more real and more concrete, something touching not only the mind but the heart. These people dedicated themselves more and more to certain mystery cults. There was the big sweep of the different mystery cults of Mithras, or Isis, Osiris, of the Egyptian mysteries and the Eleusian mysteries, which became increasingly wide-spread with their symbolism and initiations.[7]

Alchemy naturally fits into the conscious religious and philosophical situation of the time, and the greatest alchemist of the third century is a Greek Egyptian or Egyptian Greek, Zosimos. (We don't know if he was a hellenized Egyptian or just a Greek living in Egypt.) He had a Gnostic outlook, but was also well acquainted with the Christian tradition, which was at that time not a contradiction. While simple people adhered to Christianity as the one salvation, the new light, and the different thing, certain more skeptical, intellectual, and relativistic people simply thought that Christianity was "acceptable"; it went along with Gnosticism and with Mithraism (which is why there are even inscriptions dedicated to Jesus Dionysos or to Jesus Serapis), but they could not allow that Christianity might be in complete contrast to them. Those were the educated people with their typical intellectual relativism, and Zosimos was such a man. His conscious outlook was Gnostic, but his religious passion was invested in alchemy, in the search for the mystery of the Godhead in matter. Now, one of the concepts that plays the greatest role in alchemy is that of the *prima materia*, the prime or basic matter, the one stuff from which everything else is made. People felt that if they could find out about that—and it is still a topic in modern physics—they could find the basic key of material existence. Thus, when you compare, as Jung did, all the different concepts with which they define the *prima materia*, you realize to what extent this field of research[8] fascinated the alchemists.

In the history of alchemy one has to keep in mind the double trend of the extraverted and introverted approaches. One can imagine that naturally the introverts among the alchemists, for instance at the time of Zosimos, were more inclined to be interested in the mystery cults. They were those who recorded their own dreams and tried to use them and their meaning as a source of information regarding their work. The extraverts generally adhered more to the officially ruling form of thought. This continued when alchemy passed through the hands of the Arabs and Islam split into two denominations, the Sunna and the Shia. Whereas the Sunna were the orthodox, conformist, book-religion people, the Shia had a more personal and mystical approach and relied more on inner initiation or, as we would say, on their own individuation.

The introverted alchemist connected more with the Shia and the extraverted alchemist more with the Sunna. The great author Mohammed ibn Umail was a Shiite whose best friend was burnt as a Shiite martyr. If one reads Holmyard's *Alchemy*,[9] which uses an extraverted approach, one finds that in the Arabic tradition the great man was a Sunnite, Al-Razi. He has the merit of moving chemical science a great step ahead by developing what Jabir (a mystical imam of the Ismaili sect) called "the Science of the Balance." Al-Razi discovered that the *quantity* of materials used made also a *qualitative* difference. From then on good recipes gave more precise definitions, saying how many pounds of that substance had to be mixed with so many pounds of another to make a good amalgamation or alloy.

When alchemy reached the West, the same bifurcation occurred again among the monks and the scholastic philosophers interested in alchemy. An extravert like Albert the Great adopted more the chemical side, while the author of *Aurora Consurgens* (whom I believe to be Saint Thomas Aquinas), an introvert, assimilated more the mystical aspects of alchemy, quoting with preference Mohammed ibn Umail. The mystics among the medieval monks pounced on the Shiite text and the Platonic traditions in the philosophical aspects of alchemy, while the extraverts tried to assimilate the information obtained from Al-Razi and were more interested in the building of furnaces or in technicalities and exact recipes and their understanding.

In addition to the *prima materia*, space, time, and particle energy, one of the basic concepts of alchemy is the concept of what one might call chemical affinity, which at that time was understood as the inexplicable attraction of certain substances to one another and the inexplicable repulsion of others. This meant that a chemical substance was assessed by its value in effecting certain combinations or amalgamations—hence the famous motif of the *coniunctio*. Again the introverted mystical tradition quite naturally assimilated the religious and archetypal representation of the secret marriage of the soul with God, or of man with divine wisdom. In Islam, the biblical Song of Songs already became one of the great alchemical textbooks expressing the history of love union in a religious sense.

In order to understand the merits of alchemy and not get caught up in the modern tendency to dismiss it with the remark that medieval alchemists knew nothing of chemistry, one has to try to visualize the situation at that time with one's own imagination and let one's feelings go back to that situation. For instance, take a man who from early boyhood has asked himself what an outer thing really is. What *is* a stone? Does a stone have a soul? What is its real essence? He may try to get information from books. In Rome and in certain other centers there were libraries and bookshops, but it was practically impossible to get books on chemistry if you lived somewhat outside of town, and if luckily you got hold of one, you would find recipes like, "Mix the divine, three pounds of it, with the arsenic, two pounds of it, and then make sure that the astrological constellation is right. Then, if you pray to God and have purified your house, you may be patient, for the great union will come off." You had to work your way through all that language and try to understand it. Furthermore, overcrowded lodgings and the fear of an outbreak of fire forced the alchemist to build his furnace outside, also as a protection against curious inquisitors. So you had to buy a plot of land in a forest and build your furnace there and hire servants ready to swear that they would not tell anyone about your activities. Then the rumor would go around that you were a black magician and conjuring demons, and that if the police did not forbid this you would destroy the country. So you bribed the local police or the duke or ruler with lots of money (if you still had any left). Then they left you alone for your scientific experiments. Afterward you had to get the *prima materia* and find out where to get gold, or whatever you needed to start with. Then you had to build the vessel: go to a potter and order certain vessels capable of standing great heat. At that time such vessels could not be produced as they can be today, so people used thermoses which were simply heated day and night with charcoal or wood, and then they had to discover the technique for blowing air into the fire to get higher temperatures. Thus you had to hire some simpleton who was willing to stay awake day and night to blow the blowers so as to get the heat, and if the chap went off to have a beer your whole experiment was ruined, and you had to begin again.

I am not fantasizing. You can read about it in alchemical books, where it says, "See that your fire never goes out. . . . otherwise you can start again." That must be taken in its double meaning, for it is both psychologically and literally true.

Another great danger that loomed over every alchemist was that impoverished rulers always thought, "If only I could catch that man and make him make gold so that I could fill my state coffers." Alchemists were very often kidnapped and tortured so that they could be forced to make gold in some mystical, magical way, or to counterfeit money to save some bankrupt ruler. Thus many treatises give the warning: "For God's sake stay away, remain unknown, keep your activities secret, so that you do not fall into the hands of rapacious rulers."

Then, last but not least, there were of course people who pretended to be alchemists and quite consciously made counterfeit money and gold. They made a cheap kind of bronze legation with a bit of coloring such as is still done. This accounts for the tradition about the making of imitation gold and counterfeit money that pervades all of alchemy. This was practiced by the crooks who pretended that the world expected this of alchemists, and some of them were weak enough characters to say that this was what the world wanted from them and they were going to deliver it and make a career for themselves. That is why all the true scientists, the true searchers among the alchemists, said, "I am not looking for the gold of the ordinary people, I am not looking for vulgar gold. I am seeking a higher gold, the true gold."

Some did actually try to make literal gold, but these wanted to discover in themselves, as in matter, the mystery of transformation. We now know that it is possible: one *can* make gold from other metals. The dream of the alchemists has come true in the twentieth century, but it does not pay. It is too expensive. Yet even if the true or the honest alchemists, as I would call them, did try to do this, their reason was that they wanted to discover the underlying scientific principle. Modern science has confirmed their intuition.

So you see how expensive it was, economically and psychologically, to be an alchemist. You became a very lonely person and were looked on as a sort of sorcerer or black magician or, better yet, not even noticed if you hid completely and worked in the night and had some other profession in the daytime. It really was mostly underground work. Sometimes, however—as for instance in the Arabic period of Sheikh Al-Mamoun—certain Arab rulers and, later in Europe, abbots or higher bishops or members of the Church hierarchy or worldly rulers became interested in alchemy and supported serious alchemists in their investigations. They had no intention of forcing them to make money but were themselves passionately interested and involved, and helped others along. For the adept many other dangers were lurking. Imagine you are such an alchemist. You are sitting one evening over your books, trying to translate a phrase or to understand what another alchemist has written. Then someone knocks at the door and a vagabond comes in and says, "I hear you are interested in alchemy. Look at what I have here." And he throws a lump of ore shining like gold onto your table. You ask what it is and are told it is very valuable. So you buy it from that chap but have not the foggiest idea what it is. You turn it around and put it in the furnace, and when it is very hot something trickles out of it, and if you stick your nose a bit closer you suddenly feel terribly sick and drop half dead and lie for days in a delirium and in a toxic state. If and when you recover, you go back to your laboratory and think that what you bought must have given you lead poisoning. Thus one reads in old texts that "lead contains a dangerous spirit which makes people manic or crazy. Beware of the spirit of lead in the work." That is not only a psychological truth. Lead as a symbol is connected with Saturn, with the spirit of depression. But the hook for the projection that lead is the devil, that it contains the devil and a mania-producing spirit, is also a concrete chemical fact. If you go back in history, the psychic factor and the material factor were absolutely one, and when you read the texts you have to read them in a double way: when you read that lead contains a mania-producing evil spirit, it also means that lead is poisonous. That is why they say that Mercury—in the sense of quicksilver mercury poisoning—is an evil spirit that can completely confuse you.

Working with unknown materials, you risked developing rashes, getting sick, or becoming delirious. This is why one reads in certain treatises of the "many who have perished in our work." Again, that is not only psychologically true. Many were the victims of their experiments, for they did not know what they were dealing with.

So you see, *that* was the situation of an alchemist. He was an underground man who, out of a secret personal passion, sought the secrets of God by which He had made this whole wondrous cosmic world in which we generally find ourselves so greatly puzzled. The alchemist gave his lifeblood and money and devotion to experimenting, to finding out what the nature of these various substances might be, and at the same time he tried to understand the obscure language of his own dreams and to go on groping in the dark. Naturally, whenever we are confronted with the unknown, the unconscious imagination projects hypothetical archetypal images.

So the artist worked with his dreams and his archetypal, hypothetical representations to find out more about this mystery.

People who read Jung's *Psychology and Alchemy* or the *Mysterium Coniunctionis* and complain that it is difficult reading are actually most ungrateful. You should see the original literature from which Jung extracted these works, the dung heap from which he extracted the gold to be found in his books. You have to read pages and pages of blah-blah or unintelligible stuff to find a psychologically understandable sentence once in a while. There is only one method: confront a large number of writings. In one text you may read of *theion* and not know if it is sulphur or the divine, or something else. The best way, then, is to read everything you can find regarding treatises on the *theion*, after which you make a list: "So-and-So says that *theion* is that." Then you get an idea as to what it approximately means.

Jung did that. He brought together the greatest collection of alchemical books in the whole world, for at the time he became interested in alchemy you could still buy marvelous treatises inexpensively. Through Jung it became fashionable to collect books on alchemy. He collected all the books and then made a synoptic register, by writing down "sulphur," "arsenic," and so on, collecting references throughout all the alchemical literature. In small handwriting, chiefly in abbreviated Latin, he put all these notes together like a synoptic view of the Bible, where one can compare, for instance, what Christ said about Sophia in the gospels of Luke and Mark. This method had already been used by ancient writers, who said, "One book opens the other. Read many books and compare them throughout and then you get the meaning. By reading one book alone you cannot get it, you cannot otherwise decipher it."

I find it difficult to comment on alchemical texts, because one cannot say or find anything important that Jung has not already said. The few texts he does not mention in his writings are mostly worthless. I have not yet found any relevant or interesting passage of an alchemical text from which Jung has not already extracted the essence. For this reason I have decided here to take one of the interesting alchemists and go through his texts as a whole in order to give as close as possible an impression of the original material and context.

I have chosen the text of an alchemist called Gerhard Dorn, who must have lived in the second half of the sixteenth century. His exact date of birth is not known, nor the exact date of his death, but his main publications appeared between 1565 and 1578. We also know that he was a physician, a general practitioner, and that he was an adherent and passionate pupil and defender of his master, Paracelsus. He also advanced pharmacology to a certain extent because, unlike most general practitioners at that time, he did not only use herbal medicines. One of his extraverted pharmacological contributions was the discovery that if certain chemical medicines were applied in a refined way, if they were better distilled, they then had a better and more heightened effect. Dorn was an introvert and a very religious man, and if you have read the last chapters of *Mysterium Coniunctionis*, where Jung quotes him and comments upon his work, you know that he also tried in an absolutely genuine way to practice active imagination. He tried to talk with the things he was dealing with. I am going to tell you about one of the texts from this part of his work.

Jung sometimes defined the introverted psychological tradition in alchemy as the art of active imagination with material. We generally think of active imagination as talking to our own personified complexes, and trying in our imagination and fantasies to personify certain of our complexes and then have it out with them, allowing the ego complexes or the ego to talk to these inner factors. As you know, you can also do active imagination through musical improvisation or through painting, producing your unconscious material in the form of a painted fantasy; or by sculpting or dancing. You can lend very different means of self-expression to the unconscious. With your body you can dance a fantasy, or with a brush you can paint a weird image. So why couldn't you project your unconscious onto a chemical material and produce your fantasy with that? Why, instead of putting a mosaic together with a fantasy image to express your unconscious situation, could you not take different materials which seem to express something in yourself and mix *them* together? So that was an introverted aspect of alchemy, and naturally, while meditating on these factors, you can talk to them.

I remember when I was ten years old, growing up in the country, I frequently used to play alone in a little garden house attached to the henhouse. Once I read in a paper for young people, which gave some information on natural science, that amber was really resin that came from old trees and had been washed about in the sea. That somehow triggered my fantasy, and I thought that now I wanted to make a yellow amber pearl. That was true alchemical thinking, though I had not the foggiest idea of alchemy. So then I thought, "Well, nature makes amber by rolling about resin in the sea, so we must speed up the process of nature." (You read that in every alchemical text: "We are speeding up the natural processes.") I had not the faintest idea what to do but went about it completely naively. I thought that seawater consisted of water with salt and iodine, so I just took salt from the kitchen and iodine from my parents' medicine cabinet and mixed them without caring about the quantities. Then I collected resin from the neighboring trees, which naturally was full of dirt— bits of bark and so on. So I thought (and this again was alchemy without my knowing it) that before you mix the substances, you must purify them separately. The seawater was clean, but now the resin had to be melted and then put through a sieve. While I was melting it in a stolen pan, I was filled with pity for it and wondered if it was suffering pain. I thought that if you cooked a human he would be in agony, and I wondered if matter really was dead or if the resin suffered when I heated it. So I talked to it. I said, "Look here, you may suffer great tortures, but you will become such a beautiful yellow amber pearl that it is worth going through the torture."

Well, there came a sad end to the experiment, as often happened to alchemists. The whole thing caught fire and I burnt my eyebrows, and thus my parents found out what I was doing and unfortunately put a stop to my alchemy. Only later, when I was nineteen or twenty and had met Jung and he told me to look up certain alchemical texts for him, did I discover that I had done an archetypal thing which was right there in the whole history of alchemy. It was one of those instances where you see the spontaneous reappearance of an archetypal situation, for in my parents' library at that time there was not one book with a single allusion to alchemy in it. I could not even have heard about it by cryptomnesia. And in my Swiss village school, in the lower elementary classes, one would not hear about pearl-making or alchemy either. You could call it a piece of active, or rather, at the time, passive imagination, but an imagination making a fantasy-play with the material—not by painting a golden pearl but by making one. That was what happened to those alchemists, they were seized on an inner and outer level by the archetype of transformation—for alchemists gave themselves totally to the Great Art.

Now, you see, if you think of an archetypal motif and of an archetypal background, such as appears very often in myths and fairy tales,[10] people get caught in a trap. They enter a castle and the door shuts behind them, and that always means that now they are in the Self. Now they have reached that point in their psyche where they can no longer run away from themselves. Now they are in for it, and the ego, which always flirts with the idea of getting away from what it ought to do, knows that it is caught in the mousetrap and hitherto has to fulfill the requirements of the Self and will not be released before that is accomplished.

In all fairy tales and mythological patterns one is always released again, in spite of everything, but only after one has done the heroic deed. Trying to run away is no good, for you cannot escape. There is, for instance, a Persian story[11] where the hero gets into a magic bath in which the water rises inexorably. The hero swims until he is exhausted, until finally the water lifts him up to the level of the cupola over the bath. At that point he touches the round stone and escapes. Everything disappears, and he suddenly finds himself walking freely in the desert, towards a new, unknown trial. In 1926 Jung had the dream which he relates in *Memories, Dreams, Reflections:*[12] He was in a light cart led by a little peasant taking him to a castle of the seventeenth century. The gates closed on him. He knew then that he would be a prisoner in this castle for many years. It was when studying alchemical texts later that he realized what his dream had meant—that he was condemned to study and develop this discarded tradition "from the very beginning." It was in the seventeenth century that alchemy began to perish. The introverted approach in alchemy shows that it is just as much an investigation of the collective unconscious as of matter. In this purely psychological trend in alchemical symbolism, we can recognize what we are doing when we experiment with the unknown objective, basic layer of our own makeup. Many alchemists practiced spontaneously what Jung discovered before knowing alchemy and what he called "active imagination."[13]

# 2

### ❊

# DIVINE POWER IN MATTER

IN CHAPTER 1 I TRIED to give you a short historical sketch of the origins of alchemy, of its development, and of the role it plays in general in our historical background. Before I now move on to the special text I have selected, I want to touch on one problem that I have so far scarcely mentioned: alchemy's relationship to Christianity. You will see later that this plays a central role in the ideas of Gerhard Dorn and in the problem he faced. I have already pointed out that in the Arabic world, interest in alchemy was upheld more by the Shiite denomination, that is to say, the more introverted and individualistic Muslims, and that in the Jewish tradition it was the Kabbalist and the Hasidic movements that were more interested in alchemy than the Talmudic schools. Also, in Christianity it was mainly the monks—first the medicant orders, some Dominicans, and later Franciscans—who were more interested in alchemy when it came back into the Western world via Spain and Sicily. With it came also some unofficial Christian-Hermetic movements, generally summed up nowadays as pre-Reformation movements. These were mainly concerned with the third person of the Trinity, the Holy Ghost. In these movements the tendency was, even if the official body or doctrine of the Church was against such practice, for the individual to try to relate to the Holy Ghost through dreams, inner visions, and personal revelations. Some of these Holy Ghost movements survived and formed what one might call a left-wing movement within the Catholic Church itself, while others were excluded and their members condemned and persecuted. Many of these people showed an affinity for alchemical preoccupations and ideas. Whereas clerics maintained an interest in alchemy, these people rather tried to free it from religious implications and slowly enable it to become a purely natural science, in the modern sense of the word. In that way one observes, in general, what Jung points out in his introduction to *Psychology and Alchemy:* that alchemy was never hostile to the prevailing religious ideas and movements but rather formed a kind of complementary undercurrent. Naturally, however, some alchemists had basic ideas about God and the world and the Holy Ghost which did not conform to a strictly dogmatic outlook, but being scientists and practitioners, they usually did not even realize this. If asked, they would have said with honest conviction that they were faithful Christians or Muslims: they were not aware that by their willingness to receive what we now would call direct inspiration from the collective unconscious, they had put themselves in a dangerous position vis-á-vis prevailing religious organizations. In that way they were in a similar situation to many mystics who themselves felt that with their inner experience they were close to the very essence of Islam or Christianity, while those who knew of religion only through books and thought that that was all there was to it tried to persecute them as sectarians and heretics. This exemplifies the tendency in the official Christian doctrine to belittle any kind of personal inner religious life; one must simply believe in the historical figure of Jesus and in the dogmatic tradition about Him, and not get one's orientation on religious matters from what the clerics would call a purely subjective factor. In that way Christianity expresses the truth of the soul but in an outer, a projected form.

In his introduction to *Psychology and Alchemy,* Jung says:

27

An exclusively religious projection may rob the soul of
its values so that through sheer inanition it becomes in-
capable of further development and gets stuck in an unconscious state. At the same time it falls victim to the
delusion that the cause of all disaster lies outside, and
people no longer stop to ask themselves how far it is
their own doing. So insignificant does the soul seem that
it is regarded as hardly capable of evil, much less of
good. But if the soul no longer has any part to play,
religious life congeals into externals and formalities.
However we may picture the relationship between God
and soul, one thing is certain: that the soul cannot be
"nothing but." On the contrary it has the dignity of an
entity endowed with, and conscious of, a relationship to
Deity.[14]

In speaking of the importance of the soul, Jung then naturally uses the word *soul* in its Christian sense and does not
make a distinction between ego-consciousness and the unconscious; what he refers to is naturally that soul which we would
call the objective psyche, the deeper layers of the unconscious.
Jung then approaches another problem, the one problem that
Christianity discouraged at a certain point of its development
(as it partly still does): any inner personal life and any attempt
to rely on one's personal inner psychological knowledge, on
anything that one's objective soul might tell them. People are
taught that they should just believe what is ordered by the
Church, as though the Church expresses the truth of the soul.
This propagation goes on in the form of a projection. The
other question with which Jung deals in his introduction, and
which I shall only want to remind you, is the problem of evil.

Christianity has made the antinomy of good and evil
into a world problem and by formulating the conflict
dogmatically [for instance, by fixing what is evil and
what is good], has raised it to an absolute principle. Into
this as yet unresolved conflict the Christian is cast as a

protagonist of good, a fellow player in the world drama
[as was also the case with Manicheism]. Understood in
its deeper sense, being Christ's follower means suffering
such as is unendurable to the great majority of mankind.
Consequently the example of Christ is in reality followed either with reservation or not at all, and the
Church is forced into an obligation to "lighten the yoke
of Christ."15

In other words, practically nobody can really live up to the
ethical demands of Christianity in practical life. And through
that and by it is implied the fact that Christianity is a purely
patriarchal religion.

Jung then moves on to the fact that the Trinity is based
on the symbolism of the masculine number three, while alchemy tends to hold a quartenarian view of a Deity, four
being a feminine number. He concludes the passage as follows:

The Trinity is therefore a decidedly masculine deity, of
which the androgyny of Christ and the special position
and veneration accorded to the Mother of God are not
the real equivalent. [They are a slight concession, so to
speak, to the feminine side, but not a real equivalent.]
With this statement, which may strike the reader as pe-
culiar, we come to one of the central axioms of alchemy,
namely, the saying of Maria Prophetissa: "One becomes
two, two becomes three, and out of the third comes the
one as the fourth." As the reader has already seen from
its title, this book is concerned with a psychological
meaning of alchemy. . . . Until quite recently science was
interested only in the part that alchemy played in the
history of chemistry. . . . The importance of alchemy for
the historical development of chemistry is obvious, but
its cultural importance is still so little known that it
seems almost impossible to say in a few words wherein
that consisted. In this introduction, therefore, I have attempted to outline the religious and psychological problems. . . . The point is that alchemy is rather like an

undercurrent to the Christianity that ruled on the surface. It is to this surface as the dream is to consciousness,
and just as the dream compensates the conflicts of the
conscious mind, so alchemy endeavors to fill in the gaps
left by the Christian tension of opposites. Perhaps the
most pregnant expression of this is the axiom of Maria
Prophetissa quoted above. . . . In this aphorism the un-
even numbers of Christian dogma are interpolated between the even numbers which signify the female
principle, earth, the regions under the earth, and evil
itself. These are personified by the *serpens mercurii*, the
dragon that creates and destroys itself and also represents the *prima materia.* . . .

The historical shift in the world's consciousness
towards the masculine is compensated by the chthonic
femininity of the unconscious. In certain pre-Christian
religions the male principle had already been differenti-
ated in the father-son specification [for instance, in
Egypt], a change which was to be of the utmost importance for Christianity. Were the unconscious merely
complementary, this change of consciousness would
have been accompanied by the production of a mother
and a daughter, for which the necessary material lay
ready to hand in the myth of Demeter and Persephone.
But, as alchemy shows, the unconscious chose rather the
Cybele-Attis type in the form of the *prima materia* and
the *filius macrocosmi,* thus proving that it is not complementary but compensatory. This goes to show that the
unconscious does not simply act *contrary* to the conscious mind [which also would mean that the chemical
symbolism is simply opposite to the Christian dogma,
contrary to the conscious mind] but *modifies* it more in
the manner of an opponent or partner. The son type
does not call up a daughter as a complementary image
from the depth of the "chthonic" unconscious—it calls
up another son. This remarkable fact would seem to be
connected with the incarnation in our earthly human
nature of a purely spiritual God, brought about by the

Holy Ghost impregnating the womb of the Blessed Virgin. Thus, the higher, the spiritual, the masculine inclines to the lower, the earthly, the feminine; and accordingly, the mother, who was anterior to the world of the father, accommodates herself to the male principle and, with the aid of the human spirit (alchemy or "the philosophy") produces a son—not the antithesis of Christ but rather His chthonic counterpart, not a divine man but a fabulous being conforming to the nature of the primordial mother. And just as the redemption of man-the-microcosm is the task of the "upper" son, so the "lower" son has the function of a *salvator macrocosmi.*[16]

I have quoted this passage because it formulates in clear words what the alchemists all constantly felt but somehow did not dare to formulate to themselves. They lived out this myth, so to speak, but with very few exceptions they never were quite clear about the relationship of what they were doing to Christianity.

One could say that in this undercurrent of alchemy versus the official Christian dogma were the beginnings of what we now call the split between religion and natural science. As a kind of general cultural slogan, this is currently discussed at length and generally solved with stupid and well-meaning phrases and generalizations. Many scientists, for instance, carry on their practical work—study genetics, or whatever it may be—with a purely materialistic outlook, while on Sundays they still profess in an awkward kind of way to be Christian, but they would not like to have the two things compared too closely within their own psyche. One could therefore say that is one of the great splits in our modern civilization, bringing about tension between the alchemical and the Christian symbolisms. But the alchemists could still keep the opposites together through their slightly sloppy way of thinking, and also because they were in the fortunate position of projecting their main preoccupation into matter, so that it did not concern them personally—it was something which took place in the retort, not quite in themselves.

The seventeenth century was the crucial moment when alchemy split off and became a purely extraverted natural science. At the same time another problem arose, for in the undercurrent of alchemy and the layer of the Christian dogma were two very different trends. Slowly, in this same century, the realization emerged that alchemy was also a religious problem, and the two layers approached each other. Where this fact was simply ignored and discarded, people just went on courageously with what they called pure science, with no more discussion of the Holy Ghost and God—*that* was all nonsense and had nothing to do with chemistry, which was a purely practical science. Religion was put on the back shelf for Sundays. Other people, however, saw or at least got a glimmer of what Jung rediscovered, namely that alchemy implies a lot of experience that belongs in the realm of religion.[17] To meet this, such people simply discarded what was undogmatic in alchemy and assimilated it into the Christian conscious view and made out of alchemy a kind of allegorical moral teaching.

The clearest exposition of such views is to be found in the writings of Johann Valentinus Andreae, who was probably a southern German parson, and who wrote under the pseudonym Christian Rosencreutz. He was the founder of the Rosicrucian movement. From the body of alchemical symbolism and tradition he extracted everything which was not in strict contrast to Christianity and transformed it into a kind of moralistic, well-meaning Christian allegory, doctrine, and symbolism. It is to be found even more clearly in the traditions of the Freemasons.

Thus alchemy partly got absorbed into the Christian consciousness of the seventeenth and eighteenth centuries, and lost its basis as an immediate experience. It evolved into literary aestheticism and became basically a kind of watered-down moralistic teaching which one still finds among the Freemasons. There is a whole tradition of so-called alchemical literature even now in England, where there are people who are still adepts and devoted to alchemy; they have, however, completely lost the relationship with the experimental science of chemistry, and with it, the whole individual drama of really experimenting with the unknown; it has become a mirror image of certain Christian doctrines, even though the Freemasons were originally against the Catholic Church.

Thus the tradition of alchemy got assimilated into the new collective consciousness and lost its genuine independence, which naturally had had its basis in experiments with the unknown. I mention this because Dorn was just such a person; he was just on the verge of that. He was one of the few introverted alchemists at the end of the sixteenth century who realized that alchemical symbolism and tradition implied a religious problem. Therefore, in contrast to many other authors, he "had it out" with it; he asked himself whether what he was saying was not pagan or heretical. He made a valiant effort to integrate his former Paracelsic teaching into Christian ideas. Naturally, for him too there was no question of discarding his Christian weltanschauung, so he tried to fit it into the Paracelsic teaching. He really pursued the problem that, in a sovereign way, Paracelsus, the teacher whom he so much admired, had ignored. Paracelsus had not bothered about such silly details; he simply said, "I am a good Catholic," and went on happily in an utterly pagan way—but with such good faith, honesty, and *élan vital* that he got away with it. But Dorn had a more introverted and reflecting nature and was also more of a systematic thinker than the obviously wildly intuitive Paracelsus. Dorn became aware that they had all talked to matter in necromancy, pyromancy, astrology, and so on—and how did that fit into the Christian dogma?

You will see, therefore, that in Dorn's writings there is a huge problem, that of the three and the four, which Jung alludes to in his introduction. The problems of the feminine and of the body were great problems for Dorn, and his conscious plan was, to put it strongly, to castrate alchemy, as later the Freemasons and Rosicrucians did, and make it artificially fit into his conscious weltanschauung. Thus in a way he was one of those sinners. On the other hand, he was still genuinely fascinated by this mystery, and as a physician and pharmacologist he was still really experimenting, and therefore did not quite succeed in just rethinking the alchemical tradition and rebuilding it, giving it a kind of conventional Christian outlook; he got stuck in the conflict which he never resolved, even though he tried to in all sorts of ways. You will see how he fought with this conflict and how he tried to find a solution. Also as a practicing physician he could not, like the parson Andreae, completely overlook the material aspect of man, that is to say, the body and real life.

No general practitioner can ignore the importance of the body or the effect of physical chemistry on human life; neither can he ignore all its seamy and less elegant aspects. Even at that time, just as today, he was pulled into the intrigues and love stories of the village in which he practiced, and he had to know the dark side of life if he really were to deal with his patients properly. A physician is told so many lies and is pulled into so many things that he cannot indulge in benevolent, highfalutin illusions, such as parsons sometimes try to build up (to their own detriment) about the true nature of man.

So Dorn was not blind to the dark, chthonic feminine aspect of alchemy, for he had fought with that problem all his life and had come to certain personal solutions that he tried to build up, but with a prevailing, consciously Christian trend. You must therefore not be shocked, though you might be slightly disgusted, because our text will contain very churchy and pious passages where he gives rein to some Sunday preaching that has very little to do with the alchemical background. If, however, you understand this, you will see how he just tried to hold on to his conscious views and thereby suffered an inner conflict.

This man was going through a real religious conflict between Christianity on the one side and alchemy on the other, to which he tried to find his own personal solutions. I have already mentioned that we know practically nothing or very little about Dorn. He was general practitioner in southern

Germany. Most of his works are dedicated to dukes and arch-dukes—the Austrian archdukes and the Prince of Baden—so he must have been well known. He seems to have extended his practice as far as the courts. He edited twenty-six of Para-celsus's treatises in Latin translation and published them in 1575 through the famous publishing house of Perna. Dorn himself translated ten of these treatises from Paracelsus's German during the years 1568–1570. To some of the Paracel-sus[18] papers Dorn added his own commentaries.[19]

Dorn was always suspect to the Church because he was known to dabble in astrology, numerology, geomancy, pyro-mancy (divination by means of fire) and hydromancy (divina-tion by looking into a bowl of water). In numerology the idea was to replace every letter of the name by a numerical equiva-lent, from which, as in a horoscope, the character of a person could be told. Geomancy is a kind of astrology projected onto the earth, as the name says. I do not want to go into that; we can sum it up in general by saying that, like his teacher Paracelsus, Dorn was interested in occultism and in all the other occult arts of his time.

Now I would like to start with Dorn's writing. The first part of his treatise is called "Chemical Philosophy," and the subtitle of the second part is "Speculative Philosophy." Jung's quotations are generally taken from the latter, since it is the more interesting paper. The introduction to "Chemical Phi-losophy" is rather boring and uninteresting, but as I have made it my task to acquaint you with the whole work, I will give a summary of this also. I am using the so-called *Theatrum Chemicum*, volume 1 (Strasbourg, 1679). There are several other editions (I myself own a slightly earlier one), but this is one of the earliest complete editions. I shall try first just to give a summary of this first part of the treatise, because what Dorn says about "Chemical Philosophy" is wrapped up in a very complicated and pompous style. Afterwards we shall go on to the second part, the more interesting text.

The author begins by defining what he understands by chemical philosophy, and says:

Chemical philosophy teaches the latent forms of things according to their truth and not according to their appearance. Access to this chemical philosophy is double, namely through opinion and experiment. Through opinion you form an idea of what is to be investigated, and the experiment is the verification of the former.

So the outlook is as follows: the chemical appearance of things, of glass, for example, is not its true essence. Dorn's idea is that behind or in it is a true essence, so to speak, and that chemical philosophy deals with this, access to it being doubled by one's forming an opinion and by experimenting. It could be said that that is still the case, considering that we have theoretical physics and experimental physics. Dorn sees this double outlook in all natural sciences. By "opinion" he means forming a hypothesis, as one does for instance nowadays in theoretical physics, afterwards verifying it by experiment. There you are already at the beginnings of modern science.

Dorn then goes on:

Through study [and by that he means just reading alchemical literature] one acquires knowledge; through knowledge, love, which creates devotion; devotion creates repetition, and by making continuous repetition one creates in oneself experience, virtue, and power, through which the miraculous work is done, and the work in nature is of this quality.

Here there is a strange mixture of outer and inner factors. First, by reading the books, one acquires alchemical knowledge, through which one acquires love. Later one sees that by that he means a kind of unconscious fascination. Love means here that one suddenly begins to understand, somehow one becomes passionate about finding the truth, so that one assumes an attitude of devotion and devotes one's whole life to the investigation. One repeats the experiments and one acquires—and here it becomes very strange—a "virtue" of power through which the miraculous work is done! Now it becomes a purely inner factor, which is typical of the *mixtum compositum* that these texts always are: suddenly the author thinks of a transformation of the alchemist in himself, so to speak. Anyone who has studied alchemy for many years, who has followed the recipes and done the experiments with complete devotion and love and repetition, changes his own personality. He acquires a magical power by which he will succeed in producing a chemical transformation in the retort, which, for instance, a beginner who mixes the same elements might not achieve.

You can see that Dorn suddenly shifts to the idea that alchemy is really work that one has to do on one's own personality and does not just consist of mixing things in the retort. You do that too, but only if you transform your own personality into a magically potent one can you transform the outer materials as well.

This has long been a tradition in alchemy and was handed on to Western civilization by the writings of Avicenna, the famous Arabic philosopher Ibn Sina. In one of his writings[20] Ibn Sina confirms that through the gift of prophecy and through certain techniques of ecstasy reached by long exercises in meditation, the soul of man acquires some of God's capacity even to change material things. You see, when God said, "Let there be light," there was light, but when a man says the same thing, nothing happens. If, however, a man, through religious meditation, can get so close to God within himself that he can, so to speak, get some of the power by which God can just will or wish things and they attain material reality, then the soul acquires some of that ability. It is on that assumption that alchemical activity and transformation are based.

This point has been handed on in Western alchemy, and one sees that Dorn, a strictly introverted experimenter, picks up this thread of tradition, which belongs to the general trend of his time. He is not the only person to subscribe to such a view. The famous Giordano Bruno too believed in this and sketched a whole theory in which he showed how a man could become a magus, a magician, through inner meditative exercises. Giordano Bruno himself tried to do this by meditating on certain mandala structures, of which he drew a countless number, and recommended one special one, namely a mandala made from metals and chemical materials that one had to hang over one's bed and meditate on. Bruno pointed out that if one meditated on this chemically real mandala for years, one unified one's own inner personality and saved one's soul from extraverted distractions and dissociation. If this was done with the proper attitude, with certain exercises which he called contractions (*contractiones*, but from the way he described them, we would call them exercises in introversion), one became a potent magus, and even outer materials would begin to play a part.

Naturally, like all believers in magic, he was encouraged by experiencing actual synchronistic events. What we now call synchronicity was in the past always interpreted as a magical effect, and Bruno had such experiences and believed in such a possibility. But while Marsilio Ficino and Pico della Mirandola kept more or less away from magic, their viewpoint in general is not different. Bruno, much more of a naive genius, really put it into practice. Unfortunately, he thereby also drew the persecution of the Church onto himself.

At that time magic was partly recognized by the Church, and Campanella, a pupil of the above three, was even called on by one of the popes to carry out an alchemical, magical performance. It had been discovered that in the Pope's horoscope a very unfortunate constellation was approaching, and the Pope was terrified that on the day of this astrological constellation he would either be murdered or die. So Campanella was invited to carry out in a small Vatican chapel a kind of magical or chemical procedure, by mixing counter elements to ward off the influence of Saturn and Mars or all other negative constellations and thus protect the Pope, with the result that he survived the day. You see how in those days the

Church half-recognized such tendencies or even put them into practice. But to be as naive as Bruno and go ahead and uphold the heliocentric system and speak about many worlds, many firmaments, and so on, was going a bit too far, and he put his foot in it.

One sees therefore that if Dorn believed that one had to do alchemical work with certain introverted meditative exercises, through which one tried to influence one's own makeup and personality, he was not out of tune with the trend of his time but was on a level with the leading spirits of the Italian hermetic movements and the Renaissance in general.

In this way one acquired virtue and power. "Virtue" must not be understood in a purely moralistic sense; it had the tinge of the Latin word *virtus*, which means "energetic effectiveness," the capacity to transform things, influence, or even mana—it still has a mana aspect. At that time the root of the word *vir*—man, virility—was still in consciousness.

Then Dorn continues: "Chemists call nature the activation of heaven with the elements in the generation of all things." Now we see a bit more clearly. Before, he had said that chemistry is concerned with the form of things, and by form he meant something very opposite from what we would call form, namely, not the outer shape or form but the true, hidden essence of a thing, in a more Aristotelian sense. The "activation of the sky" which Dorn mentions corresponds to what he calls "form," as in the next sentence, where he amplifies the meaning he gives to that word.

> This form, or rather, this hidden essence of an outer material object is what the firmament [Dorn means the actual astrological constellations in heaven] has constellated within the chemical element, and it is the coming together of what one could call dead matter with that hidden influence of the elements and the astrological constellations that together produce things.

As I noted in the previous chapter, alchemical texts can only be understood by adopting synoptic views, by putting all the quotations together and then seeing intuitively what they are driving at. Dorn too can only be read in that way; one always has to keep in mind what he means by "form," then look to see where he again speaks of it, and then compare the texts. Here he describes form as the activation of heaven in lower matter. Then he continues to associate, making clear what he means by it:

> Form is the action of the ethereal region upon the elemental region. Thus nature prepares matter by including form in it like sperm in the matrix, the latter then produces like an embryo the different species of things. Matter *can* give birth.

That is of course a slight jab at the idea that matter is dead. Paracelsus contended that matter was a living counterpart of the creating deity. He was a dualist in that respect, for he did not share the official dogmatic opinion that God created matter the way it is described in Genesis. He believed that matter was uncreated.

These philosophers thought that in the beginning, when the spirit of God hovered over the abysmal *prima materia*, she was there too and was not created. There were two things in the beginning: the male father spirit and the female matrix being, the chaotic matter, matter as in *increatum*, a not created but equivalent principle from the very beginning. That is one of Paracelsus's ideas which Dorn shared without noticing that they were heretical. That is why he says with a certain emphasis, "Matter *can* give birth"—but then he corrects it:

> If form has generated in her matrix, the whole visible world is thus created and is divided into four elements. ⌈You can see that in the very beginning of the creation of matter the spiritual deity, the world creator, is seen more or less in the Christian way, which included the sperm of form.⌉ Form is the sperm of God's creativity in the dead matter of the beginning, the matrix, from which came all things.

---

So matter is a living, feminine counterpart of the spiritual creator, a deity, and not something He produced and molded according to His will. This already contains an allusion to what Jung pointed out in his introduction to *Psychology and Alchemy*, that alchemy had an outlook in which the feminine was recognized as an equivalent principle—not as something on the border, a little bit recognized on the side, but that it had the same dignity as the spiritual father creator-god. It was his feminine partner and a living principle on its own. Dorn used the word *matrix*, and the activity of the male spiritual principle, which he calls "the action of the ethereal region onto the elemental region," is what he means by form.

That is the summary of Dorn's first chapter, in which he gives his basic outlook on the outer reality of nature and his philosophical presuppositions in approaching his chemical work. He then addresses the *opus*, the alchemical work.

> The work is done through disposition and "influence." [My quotation marks.] The former comes forth in that nature, by corrupting matter, puts it into a state in which it is able to receive form. Form itself consists in the influence of the ethereal region on the elemental world.

Here the author picks up the same theme, making it more comprehensive. He thinks (as happened in the origin of the world described in Genesis) that God, as a spiritual ethereal influence, sowed the semen of form into the living principle of matter. In an alchemical work one should repeat this. Therefore, Dorn says, the coarse material thing must undergo putrefaction and corruption. If, for instance, you want to transform metals, you first have to dissolve the ore of iron and/or even boil it, that is to say, destroy its coarse outer aspect, so that it returns to its original state in which it can receive the divine influence which comes from the heavenly regions and is still potent. Once corrupted and dissolved, the astrological constellation will influence it; it will then be like a repetition of the cosmogony and one can again bring forth transformation.

Having touched this religious problem, which has to do with the power of God over matter, Dorn goes into an excursion about his own Christian views. He begins by explaining the chemical outlook, after which he seems to have told himself: "Now I must make a confession of faith," adding:

> The whole world has its form from the holy *ternarius* number three in its order and measure, because *one* is no number but is the union of peace. Number *two*, on the other hand, is the first number that can be counted and is the source and origin of strife and conflict. Through accepting or taking on a material form, *two* has cut itself off from the original oneness and can only be made to return into that through a completely solid unbreakable bond. As one can only mate similar things with similar things, and because God has pleasure only in odd numbers [you see there the masculine predominance; God enjoying the odd number is a quotation from Virgil], the *one* unites, with its simplicity, the *two* into a *three*, and gives them a soul.

Dorn means that there is a kind of chaotic original *one*, which is not even a number, it is the one and the whole. Then out of it comes the *two*, and that is the conflict. There he uses a German word, *Zwietracht*. *Zwietracht* means enmity, but it has the word *two (Zwei)* in it, and later he also brings in the word *Zweifel*, doubt, for when you doubt, then you are two. So two is the origin of all evil and is, if you remember Jung's introduction to *Psychology and Alchemy*, the state of conflict into which Christianity has put man: God and the Devil, spirit and matter, father and mother, and all the opposites. And now one should again find a bond, something that unites the opposing twos, so that they can return to oneness; that is the three. You can say that three consists of what unites the opposites, and that in a way it is a return of oneness on a higher level.[21]

Now it gets ticklish, because somebody who can think will say: "Well, is that not four? Because, after all, this three-oneness is not the same as the original oneness; so you have the original one, two, three, and the new one as the fourth." As Maria Prophetissa says: "One becomes two, two becomes three, and out of the third comes the one as the fourth." But Dorn just skips over that question, he sneaks over the problem, taking the three as the oneness, the eternal bond established between the opposing twos, which is somehow a return and an identity with the first one. Thus Dorn still tries to save his purely dogmatic Christian outlook.

> According to this there are also three kingdoms in nature: the mineral world, the world of vegetation, and the animal world [and then Dorn makes a reference to Marsilio Ficino]; accordingly, in the realm of metals too, gold consists of three elements, namely of sulphur, *mercurius* or quicksilver, and the earthly sun [meaning gold]. [Dorn then goes on to chase the *ternarius*, the three structures, through his whole universe.] . . . Thus in alchemy too we have three steps, there is the color black, the *nigredo*; the *albedo*, the whiteness; and *rubedo*, the redness; [and then Dorn cannot quite keep away from the fourth, and says:] but red is imperfect, because it is too much of an extreme color, that is why to gold is added *citrinitas*, the yellow color, which is a middle thing between white and red. [So you see we have three colors, to which yellow is added as a fourth.] Gold is a medicine which has been moderated in its original effect through the alchemical art and therefore can positively influence all other earthly and material things. [We do not yet see what Dorn is up to, but just follow him for the time being.] Gold is a form which is separated from its body.

Now we come back to the concept of form. We now see that by the word *gold* Dorn does not mean the actual metal gold, he means that divine creative something which is every-

where in matter and which is God's, the male God's creative
seed in matter, which is, so to speak, strewn or dissipated into
every material thing. It is that semen, that sperm, which could
be extracted by boiling and by destroying the outer shape of
most chemical things.

> Gold is the form which has been extracted or taken
> away again from its outer body, and it is something so
> subtle that it has an effect on every outer object, as the
> heavenly form has that effect through its virtue of unity.
> Gold is that divine seed hidden in all materials, not only
> specially in metals, but in all material objects, and it can
> be extracted or brought out by cooking and then, as
> when God originally created the world and had a cre-
> ative effect upon matter, if you extract gold in that way,
> you have that thing which repeats God's creative work,
> you have a bit of that in your hand. [As I said before,
> Giordano Bruno thought one could acquire or steal
> something of God's creativeness.] From the creativity
> stolen from God one can create and transform things.
> Gold has this virtue, because of the virtue of its oneness.
> [Dorn always talks of the form of gold as having the
> characteristic of being this one thing.] Even vegetable
> things [in other words, plants] can produce a medicine
> which one can use in that way [that means Dorn thinks
> one can start from any outer material to make that mys-
> tical gold which is a kind of subtle body]. I now want to
> go [Dorn says] to the practice of chemistry and leave
> the occult theory and give a rule, give certain instruc-
> tions, about how to build the practical stove in which
> things are distilled.

Dorn proposes to build the alchemical furnace. These
stoves have four steps and are built like mandalas. They have
four stories and form a kind of three-dimensional mandala.
Dorn means his statement completely concretely. He also
gives certain rules as to how to make the fire in these stoves
and how to build the glass retorts.

After having explained how to build this thermos or al-chemical oven which, in spite of its appearance, according to the text has four stories, Dorn goes on to say that the fire should always burn slowly and be kept low. Very many alchemists did not even have a fire but kept an even, warm temperature in their thermos by using horse manure. This heating procedure through the fermentation of the manure is taken from agriculture (hot coat).

> The opus, the work [Dorn says], consists of two basic steps: first comes the solution, the dissolution of the body; and second the coagulation or condensation of the spirit [by which we can guess he means the opening of the body to the heavenly influence by melting or evaporating it and destroying what we would call the coarse outer appearance], after which the hidden gold appears which has to be coagulated into a new body, and that would be the gold. As you remember, gold is the form separated from the body. These three simple operations are like making the quintessence of wine.

Now he compares the process of destroying the outer and coarse aspect of matter and extracting the true form to making alcohol, to getting out the spirit from the grape juice, getting its quintessence—for in a primitive way of thinking, alcohol contains the condensed essence of the nature of wine. So, he says, as you can make wine out of grape juice, you can in a similar way distill all other bodies. Thus for Dorn the whole process of alchemy is a parallel to the preparing of condensed alcohol, which, as I told you before, has a certain merit pharmacologically. Dorn first had the idea that if medicines were distilled instead of being applied in their crude form, they would be much more effective. This is still meant in an absolutely chemical sense and not only psychologically. Only when it comes to the effect of the gold form does Dorn speak of it being done by *symbolizing*. (Keep that in mind. Do not speculate as to what that is, for it is not what we would think.)

---

Once that mystical, efficient, essential something has been extracted from matter, then other matters can be magically transformed, for these are affected through symbolization. So you get a threefold medicine which heals all outer things in human beings. An individual is mainly himself a perfect mixture. If there is some deep disturbance, it is not the fault of the form, of that gold thing inside, but of matter.

Here is another association, namely, that the gold form united with matter normally produces a perfect individual consisting of a balanced mixture of all entities, and if it contains a fault, it results from matter. Why that is, you will see later.

Now we come to the third part of Dorn's first chemical philosophy, in which he tries to exemplify in his own way what he has explained here in theoretical or philosophical language. In a kind of stammering way the alchemists were trying to explain something inexplicable, and to express it they used a simile. That is what Pauli meant when he exclaimed spontaneously: "Oh, then God is left-handed after all," which was a symbolic or mythological way of expressing what the principle of imparity meant to him. Thus you see even modern physicists express what they really mean through a simile.

In the same way, Dorn now expresses through a simile what he means by the corruption of the crude outer material form and by the bringing forth of the inner spiritual form, which is gold, and says what has to be done with it.

We give that which has little value and is precious in the relationship of one to six to the dragon who carries the Aesculapian staff; then the very restless, nervous dragon becomes quiet and goes to sleep, after which two sources, two springs of white and green water, arise and flow over it and absorb it. When the next summer heat comes, the water which has drowned the dragon evaporates, and its corpse lies at the bottom of the sea. When thrown into the fire, it returns to life and resumes its wings, which it apparently had lost, and flies away. But the child conceived by absorbing the cheap precious thing is left behind in the fire. Because that child, that fetus, was born in the fire, it can nourish itself like a salamander till it has grown up. Then it becomes quite red and of blood color and has to be washed in water, which is luckier than that in which the dragon was drowned. You have to wash the mother, dipping her into the water so that sick people can be cured. [Dorn then suddenly jumps to the sick—whose bodies become pale, their soul separating from the blood, a process that overtakes all bodies.] If one then takes this soul, which has now become healthy and freed by the simplicity of its power from all its imperfections—and only the philosophers will know this—then this soul is the most complete medicine and the most simple thing. Nothing corrupt has been left in the human body; the soul revivifies everything which is sick, and transforms it into a moderate balance. The soul (or medicine) moderates everything which is without measure, and by its own innermost simplicity it creates peace between mortal enemies and gives them back into life—God willing. It even brings dead bodies back to life, and brings health back to their sick bodies.

This is an effort to show what the work is and what it says: "we give cheap and precious food to the dragon, to the caducifier" (the staff of Hermes or of Aesculapius). Chemically that would mean that we use the mystical gold, the form gold, and throw it into Mercury in the relationship of 1 to 6. That is to say, we repeat the creation of the world: namely, we take that mystical creative power of the Godhead and confront it with, or make it penetrate into, the material reality of man.

We will see later that what is meant by the material reality of man is, on the one side, our own projection onto reality (or what we like to regard as reality), but on the other hand also has to do with the human body. What would that mean? What Dorn calls the creative power of the Godhead, or that gold, would, in our Jungian psychological language, be the active emanation, the active psychological dynamism of the archetype of the Self. To insert that into the body of reality would, in our language, be that we should watch the activity of the Self within ourselves and try to make it an influence in our actual life. If for instance I have a dream that I should do something (since our hypothesis is that the dream is, so to speak, a message from the Self), that would be an activity of the archetype of the Self, and to give that to the dragon to eat would mean that I make it valid for the body of my actual physical life. Having duly interpreted my dream, I will decide whether to do this or that, from morning till evening, according to that dream. That is really the body and my real life in my surroundings, that is what I feed to what one could call my reality. Then the dragon who hitherto has been restless and nervous becomes quiet and goes to sleep.

Dorn, we will see later, has the idea that our simple nature is endowed with a certain kind of extraverted, dissociated, impulsive restlessness. Natural man always has something apelike in him; people cannot even sit quietly but wriggle and scratch. Anybody who has tried Eastern meditation knows how difficult it is even to sit still for half an hour; you cannot do it at first, either on your heels or in the lotus position. Our vitality constantly drives us to do something, and if we stop that, something within us keeps going on. Try once to think of nothing even for half a second. You cannot! You will talk to yourself, think about your problems or about what you have to do, and so on. It is the constant autonomous restlessness of the life we lead, and our willpower is insufficient to enable a simple inner life to overcome that autonomous liveliness. With the help of the Self, however, it becomes possible. Our experience meets what Dorn thinks: the experience of the Self is expressed as one's innermost soul, which is touched by the dynamic aspect of the God image. It is that which quiets and gives peace to this kind of apelike dissociated activity of our body and mind, and then suddenly two springs of water come from the depths and create a flood which covers everything with sea water, drowning the dragon. In modern psychological language we would say that through meditative concentration and introversion the unconscious begins to flow. The springs of the dream life, of the objective psyche, start flowing again in contrast to the flickering restlessness of our conscious mind, and appease it.

After a time the heat of summer comes, meaning that if you do that long enough, something will change after a while. If you have lived for a long time in complete introversion, only concentrating on your unconscious, then this flood of unconscious fantasy and dream life begins to recede, to decrease. As the text says, you find at the bottom of the sea the corpse of the dragon, which, when it meets the fire, becomes alive again, taking its wings back and flying away again. In a way, that is just its return to its former way of living, and you would say, "Yes, and so what?" For a while you have meditated and concentrated and have experienced your unconscious, and now you return to the old way of life—but that is not quite true. As Dorn says, a child remained at the bottom of the sea, where now fire prevails, a child conceived by the insertion of the gold sperm. Though the dragon escapes again, the child remains. That would mean that of this constant repetition (as Dorn says) and devoted concentration on the inner life of the soul, something is born within one, namely, a relatively constant realization of the Self.

As you all know, the experience of the Self in the beginning of analysis is generally a rare and brief moment of happy elation. One day, after having struggled with one's miseries, it happens that one feels inwardly at peace, that one has connected with one's own inner center. In Chinese terms, one is in Tao and one is happy; one feels, "Now I understand what it all means and now I have it"—but two minutes later the devil has won again, and it's all lost once more. However, the child would express that this inner experience has now become a constant presence within oneself, even if the dragon flies away again; that is to say, ordinary man gets going again with his own nonsensical thoughts and actions, but in spite of that, inwardly there is now another entity at the bottom of the soul, so to speak, which is a constant personification and realization of the Self.

This child was born in the fire, of the libido concentration on the inner world; it nourished itself like a salamander in the fire, and when grown up it became red and blood-colored. I do not want to interpret that because we will discover ourselves later what it is. The inner experience has become constant and inwardly matured. Now one has to wash it again, but this time with waters which are luckier than those in which the mother was washed. Now the mother is really the dragon, so it would mean the dragon got killed or drowned by the waters of the unconscious, while now the products of the waters, of the unconscious (which I would interpret as the flow of inner fantasy life), do not kill the child but on the contrary, have a nourishing effect. At that point, Dorn jumps to another subject—namely, sick people—so that these may live.

You should not forget that Dorn was primarily not looking to find this inner child, or the form of gold, or to be in touch with God's creativity for his own inner beatitude or salvation (though he mentions that too), but he was a passionate physician who was really seeking cures for his patients. Therefore the second time water starts flowing; it is his inner experience which he can now give to others, especially to the mentally and physically sick people around him. Dorn then described dramatically how, when that water touches other sick people, they become pale and their souls separate from their blood, because it is the soul which makes everything healthy. Having now gone through his meditative work on the dragon (which would be the unconsciousness of a human being), and having gone through death and inner resurrection, Dorn notices the effect on the surrounding sick people: first they turn pale—and their souls leave their bodies. That's a nice way of expressing that they are killed!

There is, therefore, a kind of infectious effect on other people so that they too are killed by this soul medicine, but through that process the soul becomes healthy and can return to its original state in the sick as well. Thus when the soul returns to the body, it is like a medicine which leaves nothing rotten in the human body but heals all sick people through moderation or balance. Like many general practitioners—quite rightly, even nowadays, and I am all for it—Dorn believed that a balanced way of living was the best way to keep physically healthy. Not to sleep too much, not to eat too little or too much, to have the right amount of exercise, and so on. This is a banality but it is also very true, for when people become physically ill, the illness has generally been built up by having lived for years and years without inner balance, either by overeating or not exercising or not sleeping enough; then one day nature presents the bill. Dorn, being a practitioner, was aware of that.

His gold medicine would cure the soul of people. We would call it psychological healing through getting in contact with the Self, or with the process of individuation. At the same time Dorn's method keeps the body healthy and cures it, because it induces man to lead a moderate way of life. This medicine also makes peace between enemies and gives life back to half-dead people and health to dead bodies.

Dorn concludes by saying; "This medicine which I now mention, this child, or this gold form, is really a resurrection of the Holy Ghost." He thus links up with the Christian weltanschauung.

# 3

# THE PROBLEM OF THE BODY AND THE REDEMPTION OF THE CHRISTIAN SHADOW

DORN HAS RELATED HOW THE DRAGON was first drowned in two sources of white and green water. The heat makes the water evaporate, so the dragon lies dead on the ground. Afterwards it is revived by the fire, gets its wings back and flies away, leaving back the child which was conceived through the precious thing with which the dragon had been united in the waters. So the child lives and grows in the fire like a salamander; later the child has to be washed again in even better water.

After this there is a strange skip in the text, when the bodies of the sick become pale and the people die but are revivified and resurrected by medicine.

We are going to try to translate this into our modern mythology, that is, into psychological terms. To begin with, Dorn says that what is cheap and precious is given to the dragon in the relationship of 1:6, after which the restless dragon falls asleep. First let us look at how Dorn himself amplifies the theme: for Dorn, the restless dragon is the body, but for us it would rather be something like physical man, the extraverted aspect of a man or a woman who lives in the concrete physical world and only attends to that. And by what has little value and is precious, Dorn means what we would call the Self, but since this psychological concept did not exist at that time, he describes it as the innermost divine center of the psyche. So it would mean that the divine center of the psyche, the Self, collides with, or comes together with, the restless extraverted personality, which is concentrated on outer physical things, with the result that that part of the personality, in other words, the dragon, then drowns in the unconscious.

That is exactly what happens with us. When people come into analysis, they generally have a long tale to tell about their troubles: their marriage, their profession, and so forth. Generally they say they have come into analysis for such and such reasons, and typically the reasons are based on the way in which consciousness sees the situation and on the kind of snare in which the patients believe themselves to be caught. Very few people say that they have an inner problem, and even if it is an inner problem, they describe it more as "the restless dragon." When they come to understand that the solution is to be found within their own psyche and not in the analyst or in some outer thing, the worry diminishes, the restless dragon is appeased.

One first accepts the situation as described above, but then one says, now we have to see what the person's own psyche has to say. With that the person is forced to stop worrying and to say, "Well, now I am faced with the unknown and just have to wait." Then the waters of the unconscious rise. That would be the flow of the unconscious fantasies in the night in the form of dreams and in daytime fantasies, and the entire analytic work concentrates on that. In that way everybody who starts an analysis drowns within his or her own imaginative inner activity. This way we consciously stop worrying about outer problems and solutions and put everything into a retort, so to speak. Naturally, after a while, the waters dry up a little, which means that some inner solution has been found. Afterwards there is a natural tendency to return to outer contacts and outer life.

---

Analysis is a temporary, artificial state of complete introversion which is not carried on forever. Also, the waters dry up—for instance, dream material lessens—and then the libido naturally returns to the outer world to a certain extent. There the great danger is that people may just snap back into their former way of life, forgetting all about the hot bath they had in analysis, and everything becomes as before. To a certain extent that danger always exists. But, as Dorn noticed, when analysis proceeds properly, that kind of relapse does not happen: something precious has taken place in an inner conception, which Dorn compares to an inner child. In dreams, as many of you know, this conception is often represented as a child, the Self being represented as a form of renewal.

The oneness and wholeness of the personality exists potentially at the back of the ego complex; it is its parent. But insofar as we realize the Self through a conscious effort, by concentrating on our dreams, it becomes a part of our conscious personality; in that form it is like an inner child which now nourishes itself like a salamander in the fire of emotion and keeps growing. The awareness of the importance and activities of the Self increases more and more. That the Self attracts life from the fire would mean that it attracts more and more libido.

Jung often said that when analyzing someone, one of the important things to watch is to see how much of the personality listens. Some people are very cooperative with their ego in analysis, bringing their material and making a great effort. But other parts of the personality do not listen and continue completely autonomously, as if they had never heard of psychology.

The problem is to bring all these parts into the process, and that takes a very, very long time. It may happen that even after ten years of concentrating on the process, one dreams of people who behave as if they had never heard of Jungian psychology. If then you ask yourself, "Now where did I do that?" you can make the most amazing discoveries. I noticed, for instance, that for years I had made my decisions about income tax and money problems simply based on common sense. It had never occurred to me to relate them to my inner problems. I thought that that was an outside matter to be solved by common sense, and with that prejudice I just left one part of my relationship to reality outside of analysis. That is how you can catch yourself in unconscious prejudices, saying this or that has nothing to do with the inner man, it is just a practical or a logical problem, and for logic one need not ask the unconscious; for that one uses one's own computer.

But if this child grows and becomes red and takes on the color of blood, it would mean that the realization of the Self encompasses or comprehends more and more of the life of that person, attracting more and more libido until there is a unified inner personality which permeates all activities of the conscious person. In this stage one has to wash or add more water to the matured inner content, obviously in support of what happens afterwards, for then comes this strange thought: that suddenly the red salamander-child begins to cure sick people; it becomes a kind of general medicine.

In other texts the alchemists speak of the stage where, after one has made the red king in the retort, one has to reopen the retort. There then follows the process which in classical alchemy is generally called the *multiplicatio*, a multiplying outer effect.

One can see this in two ways: one can take it quite naively and literally, namely, that a really individuated personality emanates a feeling-effect on other people by triggering within them the same process. You could attribute this to the positive, contagious effect of a personality that has become more conscious than the average crowd: involuntarily, that stimulates other people, and the less deliberate, the more effective it is. In that way other people get pulled into the healing process.

On a higher, symbolic level it would mean that . . . and now I am getting stuck, because as soon as one wants to talk about synchronicity one has no language; our European language is all causal. I wanted to say that the effectiveness of the Self increases through synchronicity, but effectiveness is a causal word. Perhaps one could say that the archetype of the Self gets into a more and more excited or activated state, whereby more and more synchronistic effects happen outside and around it which relate to it. A kind of experience takes place of the oneness of the Self with what one generally conceives, throughout one's life, to be the cosmos or the whole outer world. I observed one concrete fact, for instance, in watching Jung: the older he became, the more he got the information he needed for whatever he was thinking about or was working on; it simply "ran after" him. Once when he was occupied with a specific problem, a general practitioner in Australia sent him the complete material which he could use, and it arrived by mail precisely when he said, "Now I ought to have some observations on that kind of thing." It was as if even the collective unconscious in Australia was co-operating! One could say that this kind of coincidence is the experience of an expansion of the archetype of the Self. It is rather that we become more and more aware of the extent to which we are one with the whole of mankind and even of nature, and we begin to read it all as hieroglyphs of a writing which points to the one factor.

But here Dorn, being a doctor, is obviously more concerned as a medicine man or a shaman would be with curing sick people. Strangely enough, his medicine does not immediately cure the sick, but at first kills them, after which they get cured. This means that a personality's higher consciousness has at first a very disturbing if not destructive effect on other people. That is why the general public loathes psychology and tries to block it off with all sorts of "nothing but" reductive prejudices. The underlying, not consciously realized thought is that if one gets deeper into psychology, one will have to give up all one's present weltanschauung, thoughts, and occupations. Thus people feel threatened—and in a way they are right, they *are* threatened, because if they get in touch with their own depth, their former frame of life will collapse. Thus, in that form, medicine has a primarily destructive effect on the former framework of the personality's rational consciousness. Everybody knows that he or she has to be drowned and lie like a corpse at the bottom of the green and white water before being resurrected, but this effect goes further and ultimately cures the person. The text says, "It creates peace among mortal enemies and gives life and health back to the sick body," obviously referring to the union of the opposites appeasing the inner conflicts.

Then comes the remarkable passage that I quoted earlier, where Dorn points out that one should not seek what one needs from the outside, for we have it all with or even within us, though it does not come from us.[22] This means that it is in us—as we would say, in our unconscious—but does not come from us; the ego has not made it. If we think the ego does it, we are ready for the psychiatric clinic. Afterwards Dorn continues about the simplicity of nature. Whatever we have said so far is only a recapitulation of the first part of the work, which is called "The Speculative Philosophy" or "The Seven Degrees of the Work." First there is an introduction, which I am not quoting in detail, where Dorn points out that he is speaking of something physical and something ethical or moral, *physica et moralia*. To prevent the idea that it is pure materialistic chemistry or that it is, for instance, a purely ethical sermon in the sense of leaving out nature or the physical aspect, he says:

I am not teaching you how to make gold for money but how to find the most simple medicine, a remedy by which you can cure the sick metals of the body with metaphysical metals, and how to find a physical philosopher's stone through which the metaphysical metals transform the sick metals of the body into perfect *eleuseria metalla*, in perfect eleuserian metals.

Here Dorn uses a Paracelsian expression in which a compound word is created out of *Eleusis* (the mysteries of Eleusis) and the *Elysium*, another word for the Paradise of antiquity.

Thus the word means Eleuserian, Elysinian, paradisiacal metals. If you were to look up *Eleuseria metalla* in Paracelsus, you would find that it refers to the idea of the substances of the body being restored to their original state, to the form they had at creation. God first created the cosmos in an impeccable and complete form, and only through Adam's Fall and sin, owing to the interference of the devil, did sickness and death come into the world. So you are really redeeming the physical aspect of man by restoring him to his original state, the concrete physical state, which he had before the Fall. Dorn continues:

> Speculative philosophy [the title of this part] is a voluntary *distractio*.[23] The body must first be well disposed by moderation in life. By not eating too much, by sleeping well, walking, and so on, and by good food. Then one has artificially and voluntarily to separate from the mind, the *mens*. The body desires that which is corrupt but could not desire anything without the help of the soul, for the soul is what moves the body.

*Soul* is a difficult word, and I do not know how to translate it; perhaps it would be correct to keep the word *anima*, but then people might confuse it with Jung's idea of anima. Dorn uses the word *anima* in latin and thinks of it as female, and for the body he says *corpus*. There is also a third part in the human being, which he calls *animus* or *spiritus*, and that is the willpower to do the right thing.

Before going on with the text, I should try to explain what he means. One first has to read the whole text to see how he uses those words. By the body he understands naively what we (also naively) would primarily call the body as well, but you will later see that he also means by that the endosomatic experience of the body. For instance, later he quotes a dialogue, a quarrel between the *animus* and the body, in which the body gives its opinion of life. The body that Dorn describes must be thought of as his own body; it might be quite different in another person. Dorn's "body-person" is a pure rationalist who likes to eat and drink—a completely sober realist who says, "I only believe what I can see before my eyes, and all the rest is idealistic fantasy-junk." Also he is a passionate extravert; he only believes in what one could call outer facts. Dorn himself is an introverted thinking-intuition personality, a very idealistic person. What he calls body we would nowadays rather call the shadow; so he projects the shadow onto the body. For him the shadow dwells in and *is* the body. But he thinks of it, naturally naively, as being really his own body, and he says that the body would perhaps like to do evil, but it could not do evil if it were not moved—a corpse does not commit any sins. So the body cannot do anything evil or bad without being supported or animated by the *anima*, and by *anima*, Dorn understands a life principle that animates the body.

The *anima*, he says, is neither good nor bad. It is a neutral thing, the force or the impulse of life. Dorn even points out that all animals have an *anima*, which even implies the notion that the *anima* is just what moves one about in patterns of behavior and desires and wishes. He views it as passive and feminine; it is, for instance, one's sense perceptions and one's reactions to sense perceptions. This *anima*, a morally neutral thing neither good nor bad, stands between body and *animus*.

The *animus* for him is closer to what we would now call the ego complex, but the way he describes it, it is that which gives an impetus; it is the center of willpower in what we look upon as the ego, and he assumes that the animus is always well intentioned in life.

So now you have these three elements: first, *animus*, the ego intention of a personality, and will; then *anima*, which is passive (Dorn naturally only speaks of male psychology, because he has arrived at all those concepts by observing himself). *Anima* is what moves the body; it has and receives sensations. Third, there is the *body*, which I have already described. Now, Dorn's first idea is that these three are somewhat chaotically mixed up. They all are more or less present in life, and sometimes one or the other takes the lead. It can happen that the animus takes the lead and orders the person to do something that the body and the anima just don't want to hear about.

Now, you have to take the sword and absolutely cut those in two. You have to divorce this couple (*anima* and body) and force the *anima* to become one with the *animus*, and when they have become one, then Dorn calls them *mens*, mind. That is the *distractio*, the tearing apart. You isolate the body, so to speak, from being a part of the other two phenomena, and you tell your anima that she has to make a choice, that she cannot flirt about with those two but must choose and be completely on one side. Dorn sometimes calls this brutal act the *distractio* or describes it by the usual term in alchemy, the *separatio*, meaning separation, the cut. The body has a natural tendency to corrupt and do rather bad things, which is why the *animus* has a natural tendency to goodwill, in the ethical sense of the word, and to want to follow what in this cultural setup would correspond to the religious precepts of Christianity, as Dorn believed them.

The *anima* stands between good and evil, she is just the breath of life and is a vehicle, or an organ, of the *animus* or the spirit, just as the body is the organ of the soul. But if the anima begins to attach herself more to the animus than to the body, the two united produce a new center of the personality, the *mens*—or, as I called it, the mind, However, for Dorn this word does not have the meaning we give it. Dorn also calls it the inner man, or the *internus homo*, the man who is turned completely inward or is concentrated on the internal. If one does not succeed in building up the inner man, then one remains an exteriorized human being and an abyss of darkness. We would say that anyone who cannot bring forth this *distractio* remains in unconsciousness.

> The *animus* has pleasure in three things: in *ratio, intellectus,* and *memoria.* ⌈Take account of the fact that we are dealing with a text of the seventeenth century. We can-

not, therefore, apply our modern associations.] The *ratio*
offers the intellect the image of a speculation which he
hands on to memory, which keeps it in its secret trea-
sury. The original *ratio* is the knowledge of the eternal,
incorruptible order of the *mens*, which God received as a
present from Himself. The intellect is the organ by
which we assimilate the *ratio*, which we then hand on to
memory. There is a kind of ultimate order of the cosmos
which is also within us as the ultimate order which we
would call the Self. The order of the cosmos and the
order of the Self is the same thing. Through the *ratio* we
get a speculative image of it.

Translated into modern psychological language we would
call that order the Self, which would mean the possibility of
arriving at a creative hypothesis by looking at the inner or
outer order in nature. We look at the orderedness in nature,
which gives us first a speculative, creative idea about it. Then
*intellectus* also becomes clear, representing the comprehension
and interpretation of that creative hypothesis. Think, for instance, of the way in which a modern scientist looks at the
order of nature or observes some natural fact: through his
creative fantasy, through his *ratio*, he gets an image of how
that could be explained, after which his *intellectus*, his thinking,
his capacity to digest, to integrate the speculative hypothesis,
would store it in memory and assimilate it with other facts.
That is Dorn's definition. That is what the animus, the conscious ego, is passionately concerned with.
    Again one sees that Dorn naively projects his own think-
ing-intuitive type. So he thinks that consciousness, naturally
and passionately and with all good intentions, is exploring
the inner and outer order of things and trying to understand
them. That is true for him, and with positive intention, that
is his form of consciousness.
    He goes on:

The *anima* consists in the movements of the body and
the sense perceptions; this we have in common with the

animals. . . . Only very few people [I am skipping a bit because he becomes rather expansive here] have been able to make this first union of *animus* and *anima,* and even fewer have succeeded in the next union, namely, with that united *animus-anima,* or with that *mens,* to attend to the body's health. Such people do not recognize the goodwill of the *animus* and do not find the *mens,* the oneness of the conscious personality, and they end by going mad. Therefore first one has to unite *animus* and *anima;* when that has been accepted by the body, then from these three you can make a harmonious oneness, but it can only be done if you first make this *distractio* or *separatio.* The one is first alone, and if it remains alone it can never be united with anything else. But if it is united with something else, one has first to separate the other from the one, because otherwise it would not be one; but when the parts of the original oneness *symbolizant* [he uses here a strange and unusual Latin verb] from the one, then they can again be united.

The idea is that all these three things are really originally in a kind of unconscious oneness that first has to be cut into two, namely through this *separatio.* It is necessary to dissociate this original unity, analyze it, and make its elements conscious of one another. Then those parts have a symbolic connection but cannot talk to each other directly. You will see later what Dorn means by that. Presently I will tell you about a marvelous discussion between the *mens* and the body, where the body makes a terribly honest effort to understand the *mens* but cannot, and the *mens* calls the body a fool, which is not a very decent psychological treatment of the body. And so they just pass each other by. In the end they both say that they seem to speak a completely different language; they just do not understand each other. And then comes the "symbolization": when one speaks such different languages, one can communicate only by using symbols. At first the body cannot understand symbols but always says to stop and cease that symbolic way of talking and be concrete, for he does not understand it. But after a while he begins to understand the symbolization, and then they can be reunited in a new oneness.

> That is why first the separation or distraction, *distractio* of the *mens* from the body, is necessary, so that the later union can be achieved. Many call this *distractio* a voluntary death reached by making *animus* and *anima* one and by making them subdue the body, which has to be forced to give up his petulance, his agitation, and his constant worry about worldly things, and also his lack of moderation in his desires. This has an effect on the will. The latter starts liking this change and becomes the medicine. Then the body will condescend to join the party. [It is interesting that the body will then voluntarily condescend, growling slightly, as you will see, but he—I use the word *he* because it is a male identification of the body who speaks—will condescend to join the party.] Just as wild animals become ferocious when they eat too much, and get a cancerous tumor when they do not cleanse their bodies of all superfluous juices through the excrement, through defecation, so the philosophical medicine has to cleanse our bodies from everything that is superfluous and corrupt, and then it can cure the body.

Now you begin to understand, and later it will become much clearer. At first it looks not very different from any Christian ethical program. If you read certain medieval texts on the spiritual education of a monk, such as the *Exercitia Spiritualia* by Saint Ignatius of Loyola, you will see that some orders also have such rules as to how to overcome the desires of the body. Dorn really is referring to an ascetic exercise, and you feel that that is the same old story. But there is a very relevant difference: in the monk's introversion and meditation exercises towards Christian spiritualization, the body is entirely discarded as evil and does not later condescend to join the party. The monk has no intention of its doing so; the sooner he dies, the better, and if you die in a monastery from tuberculosis at the age of thirty, you have a better chance of becoming sanctified than if you become old and unhappy. Saint John of the Cross even said that someone who really took the imitation of Christ seriously should not live beyond forty, because Christ himself died at thirty-three. So you see that the idea of the *distractio* or the *separatio* in the Christian program is absolutely present and definite. The body is evil and belongs to the devil, the prince of this world, and you can only subdue and massacre and starve the body and throw him to the dogs—which also means, of course, a cutting off of the shadow; as you saw, the body really carries what we now would call the projection of the shadow.

In that regard, Dorn is very different, for though he shares the prejudice and hostility towards the shadow and towards what he calls the body of the earthly man, he conceives of this educational trick of subduing him by asceticism only as something temporary—to master him, so to speak—that makes a tremendous difference. Therefore, though Dorn slightly overemphasizes the spirit and has a slightly moralistic trend in his consciousness, he is a true alchemist. He thinks that the redemption of the personality as it is still conceived of in Christian terms has not gotten through to the whole person, and that even the earthly man and the physical man can take part in it and the whole of nature can join in. One need not first cut off the lower part of one's personality and then make something wonderful with the upper remaining part. He continues: "Thus, then, when the body condescends to join in, everything comes together in harmony and moderation, and then there is an ethereal substance, a balsamic substance in our body which also preserves it in a healthy form." Here it is not just a question of spiritualization and of throwing away the earthly man. Dorn even thinks that his transformation has a somatic healing effect and that this inner metamorphosis will also give the physical personality a long and healthy life. Here he anticipates what our psychosomatic medicine is now striving for: the idea that most diseases have a somatic and a psychic aspect; and that by curing the psychic disturbance, the somatic aspect of the disease can also be improved; so you have to try to cure the illness from both sides. Dorn has this same aim and says that once what we would call realization of the Self has taken place, this has a life- and health-preserving effect on our concrete physical existence.

Then Dorn makes a slight digression. Certain people, he says, ascertain that this medicine (which we would call the experience of the Self) has itself a metaphysical body; but he refuses to accept this hypothesis, because he believes that our real body, when treated properly by the *mens*, will form the basis for the medicine. Here he discards what still persists in certain traditions nowadays in Europe about an astral or a subtle body. He says in effect: "No, no, I do not believe in an astral inner body or a subtle body. I mean the real body, which has been purified, or has undergone treatment."

There you see again how much Dorn is a true alchemist, for he never allows himself to get away from the fact of the real concrete body through a trick—real concrete man as he is, with his shadow, is the object of treatment. Dorn is not just satisfied with cutting out what is disturbing in order to achieve a wonderful result with the rest.

That is something unique in alchemy; it differs, for instance, from Buddhist meditation training, for in the East there is no such return to the body (except in certain Zen Buddhist traditions). There is always the idea that certain things like worldliness, superficiality, and so on, have to be definitely eliminated, so that there is always a kind of educational program. Dorn does have a bit of that—you have to do a certain amount of it—but he always returns to the idea that the real man, as he is, is the object and even the vehicle of the inner transformation. That is where Jung, and I, agree with alchemy more than any other tradition: for if you indulge in putting away what you cannot change or transform, you will have a wonderful idealistic result that does not hold when it comes to the test.

In the next passage Dorn explains that what he calls sep-

aration or distraction, *distractio,* is simply an artificial anticipation of what normally happens at death, which is why he
also called it a voluntary anticipation of the experience of
death. Then he goes on to say:

> In the human body is hidden a certain metaphysical sub-
> stance which is known to very few people and which
> needs no medicine because it is itself the incorruptible
> medicine. The philosophers, through some divine inspi-
> ration, recognized the strength and heavenly virtue of
> this substance and how to free it from its fetters, not
> through some contrary principle like physical medicine,
> but by a similar medicine in itself.

I think that is clear. He sees the healing experience, though it
is given by God, not in some outer religious experience or
outer teaching, but in a genuine personal inner experience.
Everybody can extract the healing experience from himself.
He even says (and this is interesting, after having repeated
the scorn of the body to be found in every meditation text of
the time) that the healing medicine is in the *body,* not in the
*anima* or in the *animus.* In just that part of the personality
which most strongly resists any conscious effort, and which
we would call the shadow, is the healing medicine. It is incorruptible and has to be detected and extracted from there.

In an introvert, extraversion occurs through a kind of
naive projection. Nobody believes in the complete solidity and
the unique reality of the outer world more than the introvert,
because he has an unconscious and therefore a primitive,
strong, and naive, undifferentiated extraversion. Nobody is so
much attached to worldliness as he. Through that he is split.
Every introvert who has not gone through a long period of
analysis suffers from that. (An extravert is split too, but in
another way; I am now speaking of the introvert because our
author is one.)[24]

The introvert is very willing to see the subjective side
within himself, so far as his introversion is concerned, but

when you come close to his extraverted shadow side, you come to a naive, primitive man who always believes that the difficulty is in the outer circumstance and not in his own projections.

The idea now is that if you could find the projecting factor that comes from within that personality, then there would be the chance of unification. I gave you the example of my naiveté in thinking for years that money problems had nothing to do with psychology but had to be solved by common sense, by the means of outer reality, since money was an outer problem (I thought). However, even such a primitive, inferior extraverted part of an introverted personality can be looked at symbolically, by taking what happens in that area of life as a symbolic event; in this way it can be brought inward. Thus for the introvert it is in a way especially difficult to see through certain of the projections he makes onto the outer world. Only if he can bring them inward can he really get to the "one" of the Self, because his ego and that part of the personality can never unite except through the activation of the Self.

Dorn then ends with a short passage called "From the Philosophical Study," in which he goes into exuberant poetic praise of the goal. There he says that truth is the highest virtue and a fortress that nobody can conquer. It has only a few friends and is attacked by many enemies, nowadays even by the whole world. But it has a great inner value. Its carcass is the true philosopher's stone, the treasure that cannot be eaten by the moth or rust and that exists in eternity when everything else will be dissolved. This castle of truth has been erected to the destruction of many and to the salvation of many.

You will see later that from the Jungian standpoint the one criticism we can make of Dorn is that he does not see the dark side of the Self. He sees the ego and the shadow, but the Self too has a dark side.[25] In other words, that the image of God has a dark side he would not accept; here he is completely at one with the Christian standpoint: that God is only light and only good. But if you watch, you will see that from time to time he says things behind his own back, so to speak, such as:

> This castle of inner truth will destroy many people; it is a cheap thing, mostly despised and even hated. But one should not hate it, but rather love it; it is the greatest treasure, it is loving to everybody and hostile to everybody. You can find it everywhere, and practically nobody has ever found it. Change yourself, the heavenly wisdom says, from dead philosophical stones into living philosophical stones, because *I* am the true medicine, and I change everything which cannot exist into something eternal. Why are you possessed by madness?
>
> Through yourself but not from you [that is, within the personality but not from the ego] is everything which you need and which you wrongly seek outside. There shines in us, though dimly in darkness, the life and the light of man, a light which does not come from us [that is, not from the ego] which, however, is in us, and we must therefore find it within us. It belongs to Him who has put it into us; we can find it in Him, in His light. Therefore the truth is not to be looked for in *us* [he means the ego] but in the image of God which dwells within us; that is the one without a second. It is the Being and is in itself the whole of existence.

Dorn returns to what Jung criticizes as having been so thoroughly discarded in the official Christian teaching: namely, that every human being has at the bottom of his psyche a divine spark, a part of the Divinity that Jung calls the Self. But then all the theologians jumped down his throat. Critics from the theological camp, whether rabbis or ministers or priests, always say: "You turn religion into something which is *only* psychological." But if we have in our psyche the image of God as an active center, then we should honor our psyche as the highest thing on earth—one cannot then say "only psychologically." If the theologian says "*only* psychological," he presupposes that the psyche is "nothing but."

Dorn, being genuine, goes back to that inner image of God, saying it is there in Christianity but is never recognized. He says: "Let us take it that we have the image of God as an active entity, as an essence, in our own psyche, and then we need not run about looking for it." He takes this image seriously. To a great extent that is also true for the whole of alchemy, for the alchemist does not go in another direction or beyond Christianity, but for the first time takes Christianity in a really practical way. For the first time the alchemists try really to believe what has been preached to other people for centuries but never been believed. Dorn goes on:

> The truth is an eternal road that Adam lost in the Fall, which is why he left Paradise naked; it is the wedding dress that God will give back to Adam through His son, Jesus Christ. The truth is indissolubly combined with piety and justice, which teaches everybody to recognize or become conscious of himself—for the *mens speculativa*, the visionary mind, is higher than the scientific work.

I think that is self-explanatory; but if one tries to go deeper into the psychology of Dorn, one sees that he is questioning Aristotelian science—and there you can guess the extraverted projection.

Now comes the second degree of "The Philosophical Knowledge." Becoming conscious, or acquiring insight, is the resolution of warring opinions through the truth. Later Dorn also says that it is the resolution of doubt. Normally we all suffer from that, and he, naturally, did too. We never believe one and the same thing throughout a single day. Usually people are thrown about by moods. They listen to somebody who says that what they believe is all nonsense, and again they are convinced. Through outer influences one gets thrown about; one minute one knows something and the next minute one doubts it, and so one never really has one's weltanschauung. As one philosopher said, "In the morning I am always a Kantian, and in the evening I believe in Nietzsche!"

For Dorn, truth and also the unifying effect is the oneness (we would say the Self). The idea is that by finding the one inner truth, these doubts or other opinions get slowly dissolved. That is why he even says that resolution means putting away doubt. He seems to play with words, but it is not a play of words, he means the *solutio* in the alchemical sense of dissolving the body—the melting of the metals and the coinciding psychological state in which you take all those warring opinions and put them into an inner melting pot, out of which comes the one inner truth. Naturally, in order to find that, we have to begin with ourselves, "but nobody can become conscious of himself if he does not know *what* and not *who* he is." That is a saying of Dorn's which Jung very often quoted because it is so interesting.

One sees people—introverts, for instance—who know nothing about the reality of the unconscious but who can spend hours and hours thinking in their ego about their ego. Sometimes these people come to analysis with a tremendous consciousness of their ego character. They do know their own ego amazingly well. Of course nobody knows it completely, but such people have really honestly tried to think about themselves. Even nowadays most people still think that to become conscious of oneself means to reflect on one's own personality, just to think and brood on "How am I?" That is why people assume that analysis and psychology are all egocentric and that one should not brood on such things; one should rather help hungry mankind. But that is not what we do in analysis. To think about the ego would be completely sterile; to me that would be like the dog who tries to catch his own tail.

True knowledge of oneself is the knowledge of the objective psyche as it manifests in dreams and in the statements of the unconscious. Only by looking at dreams, for instance, can one see who one truly is; *they* tell us who we really are: that is, something which is objectively there. To meditate on that is an effort towards self-knowledge, because it is scientific and objective and not in the interest of the ego but in the interest of finding out "what I am" really. It is knowledge of the Self, of the wider, objective personality.

Dorn saw the same thing: namely that to know oneself is not to know *who* one is: for instance, Doctor So-and-So who lives in such a way and has such-and-such a character; Anybody can see that. Rather it means knowing *what* one is (that is the meaning of the word *quid* in Latin) and by that, seeing something objective, which is not identical with the subjective ego.

Dorn goes on to amplify this more clearly by saying, "on what one depends and to whom one belongs and to what end one has been created." So true self-knowledge is knowing on what one depends—the ego constantly depends on the unconscious. We depend on the unconscious every second that we function. "To whom one belongs" means where the obligation of the ego personality is. Knowing "to what end one has been created" means finding the meaning of one's life from one second to another. The end or the meaning of our lives, Dorn then says, is immortality—the state in which we constantly enjoy the presence of God. He continues:

> Everybody should carefully consider within himself what I have said before and should taste it again and again, as if drinking it again and again, and should carry it around with an honest mind. Then slowly certain sparks will come. From day to day they will come alive and alight before the inner mental eyes, and slowly those sparks will coalesce into such a light that in time one will always know what one needs and will thus only be attached to that inner truth by which great tranquillity and great quietness of mind are acquired.

We cannot approach this inner experience in a beeline. But if one meditates on the facts that Dorn has presented here, then one will always have a spark—one could say an "Aha!" reaction—and these many, many sparks of light or "Aha!" reactions will slowly become something more continuous and will consolidate into what one could call in the language of Jungian psychology a constant awareness of the Self. This exactly describes what we are trying to do. Every dream, if it is really understood, not only with the intellect but really emotionally understood, has such a shotlike "Aha!" effect upon one. If you do not have that, then you have not understood the dream yet; it has not been formulated in a way that you can accept. Every understood dream is like a slight electric shock into higher consciousness; normally one has the feeling, "Oh, now I understand," and that has a vivifying effect.

The dream one gets at night is always like a letter from the same inner center, from the Self. Every dream is that, and the writer of the letter is always the same: the Self, the one thing, the *quid*. Therefore, if you go on for a long time having these "Aha!" reactions, you slowly become aware of the nature of that nocturnal letter writer, or constantly aware of the presence and reality of the Self. That gives the ego peace of mind. If, for instance, you get into any outer jam, you may worry to a certain extent, but then you think you will wait and see what the unconscious, or the Self, says. Thus you have a second source of information. You do not always have to follow your own voice, and that gives the ego a patient attitude and a certain continuity, for it waits to hear the inner source of information through which it will cope with the impossible situation, instead of going around wriggling like a frightened mouse and thinking as the ego always tends to think: "that it has to put stalks onto cherries," as Jung once said. So the connection with the Self makes for a certain quietness and constancy in the personality.

"Learn therefore out of thyself," Dorn goes on, "whatever is between heaven and earth, so that you can then understand everything." That is what we would call the archetype of the Self and what he would call the divine image within the unconscious, which lodges in the psyche or in the body and is also a microcosm. You can learn about all outer things just as well by considering the microcosm within you.

---

Therefore, see that you become of that quality which you wish your work to be. [By that he means the alchemical work.] If you are greedy for money, then you will want your alchemical work to bring forth gold to enrich you, and your work will be accordingly. Therefore, before you start working on chemicals you must first get the right inner quality, because then you will work with that and the result will be according to what you are. Every piece of work you do accords with your own qualities. You are in everything you do; it does not depend on what you do concretely. You are in it.

That is very much like Eastern wisdom, where it is said that the right medicine in the hands of the wrong person has a wrong effect, and the wrong medicine in the hands of the right person has the right effect. It is not the *what* you do, it is *who* does the work that determines what eventuates.

Then Dorn makes a slow, conventional excursion into how God created the world and how He created Adam in Paradise and Eve from his rib. Hence he concludes that from the chaotic oneness of the personality came two, and then later those two had to be reunited. Adam was an androgynous *massa confusa* until the rib was cut out of his body to make Eve, and then they reunited and made a couple and created mankind. To Dorn the story of the creation of Adam and Eve is a simile to what he tries to explain here, for the alchemical work is an imitation of the creation of humanity, which also began with the separation of male and female.

The next chapter is called "Conversation through which the *Animus* tries to attract the Soul and the Body to him." I said earlier that Dorn had certain dramatic conversations that are very close to what we would call active imagination. It is, however, not quite the same thing because he has included his theories in them. He did not make these conversations flow completely as we do in active imagination, but thank God there is one person in this conversation, namely the Body, who obviously gives absolutely genuine answers.

Though Dorn only wants to make a philosophical "propaganda" dialogue, the unconscious plays in it genuinely from time to time and in the most amusing manner, even to the extent that sometimes the *mens*, which is supposed to know everything, gets quite upset and does not know what is wrong. Thus the conversation occasionally does turn into what we would call a real active imagination, although you have to pardon Dorn for sometimes just making propaganda for his theories and for the places where his conscious mind becomes too active.

The participants in this conversation are the Spirit, the Anima, the Body, and Philosophical Love. Philosophical Love really means love of the true philosophy, which is alchemy. This character comes only at the end; at first there are just the three. (Spiritus, by the way, is the same as Animus. Dorn is not very systematic.)

SPIRITUS: Well, then, my Soul and my Body, get up, and let us follow your guide.

ANIMUS: He wants now to go to this high place on this mountain opposite us. From its peak I will show you a double path, the bifurcation of a path about which Pythagoras already had a dim idea, but we whose eyes have been opened [by "we" he means the Christian tradition] and to whom the sun of piety and justice shows the way will not fail to find the path of truth. Now look with your eyes to the right side, so that you cannot see the vanities and superficialities on the left path, but look rather over to wisdom. Do you see the beautiful castle over there?

ANIMA AND BODY: Yes.

SPIRITUS: In it dwells Philosophical Love, from whom flows the source of living water. He who has had a sip of it will never thirst again in this dull world. From that agreeable place we must then continue directly to an even more beautiful place, which is the dwelling place of Wisdom; and there too you will find a spring of the waters which will give more blessings, for even if enemies drink of it they are forced to make peace. There are people who even try to strive higher, but they do not often succeed. There is to the north a place which mortal people may not enter if they have not previously entered a divine, immortal state, but before they really reenter it, they will have to die and throw away their earthly lives. Whoever has reached that castle has no reason to fear death anymore. Beyond these three places there is even a fourth place, which is beyond anything people can know. The first place you could call a crystal castle, but the fourth one is invisible: you will not even be able to see it before you have reached the third. It is the golden place of eternal bliss. Now look to the left side, there you see the world full of its desires and riches and everything which pleases the mortal eye. But look at the end of that path: there is a dark valley full of mist which expands to the end of the horizon—that is Hell [naturally, from the Christian standpoint].

ANIMA AND BODY: Yes, we see it.

SPIRITUS: Now we are going on this broad path [on the left path, he means, the path of Hell] and there every comfort is turned into torture without end. Do you hear how the people howl and are in despair?

ANIMA AND BODY: Yes, we hear, but will the people not return from there?

SPIRITUS: They cannot see the end of this, and that is why they just go on, and they have generally already passed the place of repentance and therefore cannot return anymore.

ANIMA AND BODY: There are also other paths in which one can get into danger.

SPIRITUS: Yes, there are two side paths which also bifurcate away from us and of which I will tell you later. Now we are going on to that place ahead, namely on those two paths, the Heaven and Hell paths, after which there are two more paths, and those are the paths of illness and poverty, which are between Heaven and Hell. They do not lead to Heaven or Hell; many people take them and then after a while illness and poverty teach them to return to the right path or may even force them to go on the path to Hell; so they are in an in-between stage of every trying and being unhappy, and one just does not know which way they will end. The broad path to the left is the way of error, and the other two paths are the ways of illness and poverty, and the path on which we are now standing, if we move over to the other side, is the path of the truth, and on the entrances to this path the angel of the Lord stands who is also called the *tractus* of the Divine. [He means by *tractus* a kind of loving attraction; we would say an unconscious fascination.] Here, even at the first path, this *tractus* attracts them all, but there are people who resist it and do not go that way, as they want to give in to their momentary impulses and desires. Those fall into physical illness, and there are only a few who through physical illness can see their error and then return to the path of truth.

Here Dorn's point of view is close to ours. Therefore he asks the same question we do: if physical illness means that something is not right in the psychic balance, then might one recover if one looked at that imbalance and corrected it? But many people do not ask that question, Dorn says, and then there are others who just continue on the way of illness and finally fall into Hell.

ANIMA AND BODY: We see a few who walk back, but only very few.

BODY: Oh no! I would rather die a hundred times than go to the end of the left path to Hell.

SPIRITUS: You talk like that because I have shown it to you, but let us wait and see if you still remember it later.

BODY (very gravely): Wherever you go, I will always follow you at once, but before we go, please tell me why we have not gone onto that other path.

SPIRITUS: There are people to whom this *tractus*—this attraction—of the image of God has been given beforehand, so that they should feel it and not go astray.

BODY: Is not everybody attracted?

SPIRITUS: Oh, yes, everybody is attracted!

BODY: But why then do they go wrong?

SPIRITUS: When they are here at the bifurcation, they turn their eyes to the left, to all these pleasures of the world, more than to the water of life on the right side and to this beautiful mountain.

BODY: What is the name of the mountain and of the river?

SPIRITUS: Both are called the first attraction of the Lord.

BODY: Are there also other attractions besides those that you mention?

SPIRITUS: There are many others in between, which people can feel in their conscience if they do not ignore it.

BODY: Why do you linger here?

SPIRITUS: To look at this divine river! Have you ever seen such a beautiful plenty of water?

# 4

## M I N D  A N D  B O D Y
## I N  T H E  C A S T L E  O F
## P H I L O S O P H I C A L  L O V E

F OR THE M OMENT the *anima* is still a bit torn and does
not quite know which side to take, whether that of the *animus*
or that of the body. The protagonists are always three in
number: *spiritus*, *anima*, and body; but when the *spiritus* or
*animus* (not the Jungian animus) and the *anima* (that which
revivifies the body) unite, they will become what Dorn calls
the *mens*. The real tension is between *animus* and body.

The discussion continues:

SPIRITUS: Did you see how we drank from the source of love,
from the spring of love at the bottom of the mountain of the
attraction of the Lord?

BODY: Did you drink?

SPIRITUS: Well, there you show how blind you are!

BODY: Well, why did you not tell me to drink some too?

SPIRITUS: Because you cannot do that until you are together
with us.

BODY: When will that be?

SPIRITUS: When you have become one with us. But first *we* have to become one, and then you will become one with us too.

BODY: And when will that be?

SPIRITUS: When we have arrived at the diamond castle.

BODY: Well, then, hurry up, because I also want to see what you see. Here, we have arrived at the first castle, and I will knock. But why are there no doors? [He does not see the door.]

SPIRITUS: Well, we, a few strangers, have come and want to ask your permission to enter. Please open.

PHILOSOPHICAL LOVE answering from within: Seldom does anybody come here. Who are you?

SPIRITUS: Three pupils of philosophy. [Philosophy is simply alchemy in this connection of thought.]

PHILOSOPHICAL LOVE: What are you seeking?

SPIRITUS: We want to learn philosophy.

PHILOSOPHICAL LOVE: Why do you want to learn once more what you have already learned?

SPIRITUS: Oh, we have only had very bad food and now we want better food. [For a while they talk about the spiritual food that they want.]

PHILOSOPHICAL LOVE: Well, I hear you have been trained to a certain extent, and in any case we never send away anybody who comes to us, so please come in, but first take off your horns before you enter the door.

SPIRITUS: All right, we will do that.

PHILOSOPHICAL LOVE: Now we always examine our new pupils.

SPIRITUS: All right, I agree.

PHILOSOPHICAL LOVE: What is philosophy?

SPIRITUS: The love of wisdom.

PHILOSOPHICAL LOVE: What is wisdom?

SPIRITUS: The highest wisdom of all, truth.

PHILOSOPHICAL LOVE: What is love?

SPIRITUS: That is the constant desire to attain the truth once one has grasped it.

PHILOSOPHICAL LOVE: Where did you learn that?

SPIRITUS: From the attraction of the Lord.

PHILOSOPHICAL LOVE: Who mediated it to you?

SPIRITUS: Those whom He taught first and who then taught the others.

PHILOSOPHICAL LOVE: But why did you not hear of that at the universities?

SPIRITUS: Oh, there we only hear of the philosophy of Aristotle and such nonsense. [There then follows a long polemic against Aristotelian scholastic philosophy.]

PHILOSOPHICAL LOVE: Well, before you come in, you must sign our guest book. What is your name?

SPIRITUS: I am called Spiritus, or Animus, and this is Anima, and this one is Corpus.

PHILOSOPHICAL LOVE: Oh, you are very close.

SPIRITUS: Oh, yes. We are three brothers.

PHILOSOPHICAL LOVE: Well, now we want first to invoke the Light, and you also have to join in. [Then Philosophical Love addresses a long, rather rhetorical, prayer to the Lord that He might enlighten the three and give them the light of His grace so that they may see the truth.]

Come in, you are now entering the door of Philosophical

Love and will learn in the school of eternal love. Let us first have a meal, but before we begin, let us pray again. [Then she* says another prayer to the Lord, asking Him to bless the meal which they are going to eat together.]

Well, Body, you can now have a meal by yourself, and eat and drink what is here, but the others I will take with me and give them different food. [And then, addressing herself to Spiritus and Anima, she says:] The Lord will now introduce you to philsophical study, but you will not be able to understand everything I shall tell you, because you are still bothered by the burden of the body. So for the moment, before you go to the original well or spring of love, it is better for me to repeat everything important. [She then gives a long general instruction on the whole problem. As it is a part which Jung quoted very often, it may sound familiar to some readers.]

Before the fall of Adam there was only this broad path on the left, and the valley of misery you saw on the other side did not exist. The blissful country was spread everywhere, but after the disobedience of the first man, God reduced this large blessed path into a very narrow one, at the entrance to which stands the cherub with a sword in his hand so as to prevent anyone from returning to home. [That is the famous story of the expulsion from Paradise.] So Adam's son turned to the left path and abandoned the one the Father had built, and built this other large path, which ends, as you remember, in Hell. But touched by pity and love, and also facing the accusation of justice, He decided to take away from the angel the sword of wrath and to replace it by a three-pronged fishing hook, and the sword He just suspended on the tree. Thus the wrath of God turned into love without really hurting justice.

But before this happened, this large river (you know that the love of philosophy did not exist yet) was not a river, or a

*Love—amor in Latin—is a masculine word, but to me it feels more feminine.

81

waterfall, as it is now, but it covered the whole earth every-where, like dew. But after the Fall it returned where it came from and became only this small river. Now, however, peace and justice have embraced each other finally from the height of this mountain, and the water of grace has come down and again touched the world. But those who go to the left only see the sword suspended on the tree. But they know its story, and because they are rooted in the world they just pass by. Others do not want to see it because they do not know about its effect, while some do not even see it at all, or pretend not to; and those all go down into the valley and are lost, unless the fishing hook catches them from behind and they become reasonable and repentant again and are partly pulled back. But in our age, which is the age of grace, the sword has turned into Christ, who for our sins went upon the tree of the cross. That is the natural law and divine grace, but now let us study the nature of the wrong path.

According to Jung, in "Answer to Job,"[26] the great prob-lem is that in the Christian teaching, all wrong comes from man and everything positive comes from God; the fact that God Himself created the snake in Paradise, which seduced man, is swept under the carpet. That God might look at His own shadow and take the guilt upon Himself, instead of ac-cusing man, has never occurred to teachers of the Christian religion. Jung compares this to a biologist, for instance, who cultivates a brood of bacteria and, if the bacteria do not behave properly, gets angry with them. Man, after all, is just a poor, unconscious creature of nature; how can one burden him with all the evil in the world? Naturally we have this teaching also, except for a small switch, at the end of the Old Testament, where God turns inwards. For once He has a moment of self-reflection and is moved to pity for man. Hitherto He had just drowned people in His rage when they disobeyed Him. In our text He faced the reproof of justice.

That is very remarkable because it suggests that suddenly divine justice accuses God Himself. God accepts that, and by or through the effect of this insight, He changes the angel of wrath into an angel of love and replaces the sword with the three-pronged hook. The rest you probably understand in light of the Christian teaching: the paradisiacal state of the world begins to fade and all the misery comes, but then, when Christ came He was not the fishing hook but the sword. Naturally, Dorn has in mind the sayings of Christ, such as: "I came not to send peace, but a sword," so you see again an unsolved problem. The three-pronged fishing hook, which Dorn would probably associate with the Trinity, is on one side, but Christ is not in it, for He brought the sword. Therefore, in spite of being the God of love and redemption, in another way He is cutting off a part of humanity, which then goes on the wrong path, into Hell.

If you look at it more closely, this whole teaching is very inconsistent. If Dorn were honest with himself, he would have to say that Christ should really have redeemed everybody and restored everything to its original state; but Dorn knows enough about the world to know that that has not happened, so Christ is suddenly shifted into the one who brings the sword and cuts the opposites apart again instead of uniting them, and his relationship to the three-pronged fishing hook remains completely unclear. That might be annoying if we looked at it with the psychological insight we have today. In what Dorn says here, there is a shifting kind of philosophy, with some slight unconscious dishonesty. But if you remember that Dorn lived in the second half of the sixteenth century, and that only afterwards came the Counter-Reformation and the age of science and the split between religion and science, then, on the contrary, one must admit that in his intuition he came amazingly close to the idea of the union of opposites. And if he naturally put more weight on the official Christian doctrine and got stuck in the dualism and split in the failure of that religion, we cannot blame him, but must rather see how much he really achieved.

Next comes a very interesting passage of instruction by

Philosophical Love, which is really a first attempt at a sociological theory.

PHILOSOPHICAL LOVE: Man then left the path of truth, and he
became naked and preoccupied with his daily worries. First
he became a peasant and so provided his food and lived by his
own work. Then followed the crafts, but through them came
inequality between craftsman and peasant, the one being
richer and better off than the other in some countries.
Through this social inequality, quarrels and distrust arose.
People began to build palaces and make wars. Everything became unstable and disordered.

Here one can recognize the seeds of the sociological theory
that developed further in Marxism, the idea that capitalism is
the root of all evil in the world. So one can even see here
something that has long been recognized: that the theories of
Marx and Engels are a continuation of certain sociological
theories that already existed in Christianity.

Philosophical Love then comments further on the way of
error:

PHILOSOPHICAL LOVE: When twenty-one years old, most
people reach the parting of the ways and have to choose between the fishing hook, by which they are attracted to the
Lord, and going their own way. But many creep under the
fishing hook or do not even notice it. The others break out
and go on the path of error and just throw themselves into a
worldly life. Then some fail and fall into poverty, and sometimes thus return to reason. The greater part, however, build
a big factory on the left path, a big building under a single
direction, ordered and ruled by work. There is even a book-
shop and a crafts workshop. [That was the beginning of the
newspapers, for which a day-and-night search for new and
sensational events goes on.] After that people even give up
their work morale, till over the bridge of illness they come to
a new stage. For this God allows such people to become ill,
but, as before, they again try to cure themselves with what

they know, and they run to a hotel on the left which is the seat of medicine, with pharmacists, surgeons, and doctors and all the medical profession [just like a sanitarium or a modern clinic], and when they are again restored to health they have become very poor [because doctors already were robbers at that time, not only today] and so they get to the next bridge of old age, still ignoring the attraction of the Lord, and only a few on this path still return to the right way. And then come the miseries of old age till they reach the last hotel, the hotel of death, and there a much more severe host receives them and kills them with the arrow of death, which separates body and soul.

The above hardly needs a comment. You see that if your goal in life is to work and make money, then finally you get ill; you have a heart attack and then over the bridge of illness you reach a real new realm and a second attraction of the Lord. It is interesting to see that already at that time (and here Dorn had the same attitude as Paracelsus) there was a strict rejection of purely physical, materialistic medicine and an awareness that at least part of the problems of illness and old age are psychological.

Then Philosophical Love goes on instructing Animus and Spiritus. The Body in the meantime is having a good meal in another room. That again is decent, for in medieval meditation texts, the body is always tortured, mortified, and abused as much as possible, treated completely as an enemy. Here he is treated not quite as an enemy but rather as a poor chap who does not understand, and he gets a decent meal in another room. He is not just mortified or rejected, as in medieval treatises like *Diligendo Deo*, or in the writings of Saint John of the Cross and others. There is a tremendous difference in the treatment of the body.

PHILOSOPHICAL LOVE: You have heard before that the sword of the angel and of the first attraction has been suspended on a tree over the shore of the river, and this sword is none other than the Son of God, the Savior of Mankind, Christ. He attracts by manifest love, not railing at those who pass by with allegories, but attracting them as a magnet attracts iron, if only the dirt and the weeds of the world do not interfere. People who admire this river, the river of divine love, and the love that is in it, and let themselves be attracted, are brought here like you, for instance, and the servants of truth accept them, as you will hear.

But before this happens, let us have some food, and then let us thank God that you came here. [Then follows another prayer.] Let us drink from this well, and after you have drunk from the well of love, you should no longer be called Animus [or rather Spiritus] and Anima; and you should also no longer be two beings, but the one Mens. [So that is the moment where this unification takes place.] When fortified like that, you can resist the hostile body apparently the body is again hostile], then you must battle with him till he has actually finished his natural course, and the *mens* will be separated from him. Later, however, it will happen that the body, too, will become purified and then will again be reunited with you in a divine mystery. But how you should fight with the body, or what that fight will be, you will hear only later, when you have reached the fourth degree of the philosophical path, namely, the frequency or repetition.

I will accompany you now a little bit and also describe the further path. Through the help of frequency or repetition, you will come to the castle of wisdom, where you will get even better food than you got here. Here I give you only milk because you are still infants. [That is an allusion to Saint Paul: "even as unto babes . . . I have fed you with milk."][27] The wine of higher spiritual instruction will come later. There virtue will teach you the fruits of love. Later will come the sixth degree of efficiency or effectiveness, which one can only find through virtue, and then comes the seventh degree, the so-called miracles, in which even the tortures of this world will become a pleasure for you. From then on it will be God Himself who guides you further, and all other company will leave you.

Apparently, after this, Philosophical Love returns to the body, who had finished his meal.

BODY: What funny company you have [he sees Philosophical Love]. Where is my *anima*?

MENS: I am here, what do you want?

BODY: I cannot see you.

MENS: Ah, now you finally admit that you are blind?

BODY: But where is the spirit?

SPIRITUS: Don't you see me? I am standing before you.

BODY: Oh, good God, two people speak out of one mouth.

MENS: Why not? Don't you remember what I told you before? That in time you will only have to fight one other person instead of being one against two.

BODY: What do I hear? Have you used magic on me and on my eyes?

MENS: Oh, I never use any magic, far be it from me, but we have drunk together from the well of love and so we have been reduced to one. Now that you have to fight two people, you really should not complain any longer, because we have completely become one: *mens*.

BODY: Well, the word *mens* has an association with many other things, because it is the beginning of many words, *mensa*, the table; *mensura*, the measure; *menses*, the months.

MENS: Oh, if only you had learned to put measure on your table, and if only you were always aware of the small number of months you have to live.

BODY: You say funny things. You know quite well that I cannot live without food.

MENS: That I know just as well as you do, but you should know that man does not live by bread alone.

BODY: What do you eat, then? I have not seen you eating yet.

MENS: Again you reveal your blindness.

BODY: In what way?

MENS: I live from every word that comes from the mouth of the Lord.

BODY: Oh, I wish to live that way too!

MENS: You will be allowed to do so sometime later on, but only after death.

BODY: You are really cruel.

MENS: No, I am promising something agreeable.

BODY: You mean that death is agreeable?

MENS: Yes, for those who understand what it is.

BODY: Please, then, describe death to me, because everybody fears it greatly.

MENS: Very well, but only you are afraid of death.

BODY: Aren't you afraid of death?

MENS: Not a bit.

BODY: With all your wisdom, you are just terribly crazy.

MENS: No, *you* are crazy.

BODY: Well, I know that everybody hates death.

MENS: Indeed.

BODY: Well, then, talk so that I can understand you.

MENS: Well, I'll explain the thing in reality, so that you can understand it.
The *mens* of man is immortal and therefore is not afraid of death, but with courage can overcome it; the body, however, is subject to death, and that is why he is frightened of it.

BODY: Well, how do you know that the *mens* does not die with the body?

MENS: I know that everything which is born of death is mortal, but what is born of life cannot die, and also that which is between life and death, namely the *anima*, will be saved unto life.

BODY: You talk completely obscurely.

MENS: No, completely clearly.

BODY: Well, what then is life?

MENS: The *anima* of the body. You remember that the *anima* is the life principle of the body.

BODY: What then is death?

MENS: The end of life.

BODY: Well, I am no wiser than I was before.

Now, if we look critically at this from our standpoint, which takes the text as active imagination, then Dorn (or the figure he represents) misses a possibility of uniting. You see, the body is really very willing to cooperate, and at a certain moment, when the two who have become one say that they are now called *mens*, instead of fighting or having silly opinions against the *mens*, he begins to associate and says, "*Mens* reminds me of many words; for instance, *mensa*, the table; *mensura*, the measure; and *menses*, the months."

If we now took this as active imagination, this very intelligent association should have been accepted. It is, by the way, an etymologically correct association, for all these words really do come from the same root, and there the body exhibits very remarkable wisdom. First, he seems to know a lot about the etymology of words, and he also touches on an essential problem. But instead of carrying on on the same track and saying to the body, "Yes, all right, *mensa, menses, mensura*, what are your further associations?," the *mens* becomes annoyed and says: "Oh, if only you had put some measure on your table [meaning on your eating]; and if only you would remember that you have only a few months to live." And then comes the whole discussion about death and so forth. But you see that Mens here is still a kind of emotional propagandist, and I would even say that here hostility starts. The body is not hostile. He is beginning to try to understand things, and if we try to translate this crucial point in the discussion into our psychological language, you will see what an important turn Mens has missed here.

If we look at what has been written on the religious life of primitive societies, it seems most likely—or at least this was Jung's opinion, which I share and which I think could in time be easily proved—that in the most primitive populations which still exist, religion consists mainly of certain rituals, which are to a great extent physical enactments: totems, meals, dances and other activities, praying gestures, and so on. A ritual like the Mass comprises vocal prayers and gestures. Man probably has never been conscious that these rituals are performed in much the same way as those of animals. From studying the behavior of animals, we know that many of the patterns of behavior of animal life do not serve (or at least one cannot prove that they serve) any immediate utilitarian purpose such as propagation of the species, eating, or survival.

Adolf Portmann explains these "rituals," as zoologists now call them, by saying that they express the meaning of the animal's existence. By performing them, it manifests its own being, or, one could say, it expresses the meaning of its existence on earth, and even the most skeptical zoologist cannot find any further practical purpose in them. If you stop animals from performing such rituals, they get sick and their vitality is lowered.[28] We may assume that even on that level already there is the need to express—let us use Portmann's expression—the meaning of one's own existence, without further practical purpose, and it is most likely that the most original and most archaic human rituals were of a similar nature.

That is also the reason why, when you go further back in the history of religion, you can no longer distinguish between play or games and rituals. The history of games such as still exist in primitive societies—like dice, ring-toss (putting a stick in the ground and then throwing a ring over it), and all the group and ball games—shows that these are played both as rituals and, at the same time, as games. In a certain part of current literature, a big discussion is being carried on, though to me the issue seems most obvious and really not puzzling. The most reasonable investigators say that one cannot make a distinction between the two things. In other words, when a man is not occupied in hunting, eating, making love, or sleeping, if he has any further energy left, then—let us use the zoological expression—he moves about and does things which to him express the meaning of his existence, and such things are generally ritual-games or game-rituals. And according to the material I have seen, at least ninety percent if not all of them always cluster around what we now would call the symbolism of the Self.

There is generally a mandala structure involved somewhere: rings have to be put over a center, or you have a round bowl into which you have to throw little stones, and you hit or miss the goal. The patterns of all those ritualistic games are bigger or smaller mandala patterns, and even the implements used, like dice, are generally of a mandala structure, and it is the same all over the world, whether in North America, India, China, Australia, and so on. These ritual games and performances are therefore the oldest features of religious life that which we can trace historically, and it really links very well with what we are now digging up from zoology. Animals have ritual games to some extent, but in man they are much more developed.

Therefore, one could say that in the original state of affairs, which can be proved historically, there is no difference between instinctual impulse and religion. Religion and the instinctual physical life are not split, and if we were to apply this to our text, it would mean that such a fight between *mens* and body did not exist in the original form; they were a complete oneness. As Jung then goes on to say, instinctual life on a primitive level is not at all simple.[29] You must not think when you use the word *instinct* that this is a kind of simple physical drive. On the contrary, it reveals itself as a complicated system of marriage class-systems, organized games, and so on. In the most primitive instinctual religious activities there is always a very strict organization involved, much stricter than in modern law. The breaking of a taboo in primitive society entails much worse punishment than any we have in our modern society, and many people, if they are not punished by the tribe for violating a taboo, either become ill or die because within themselves they feel they have failed in the whole meaning of their life by ignoring a tribal taboo.

In this way you see that the spiritual order that we associate with religious teaching and instinctual activity are in complete harmony, but again and again in the history of mankind and in the histories of religion this original oneness, or harmonious functioning of the meaning and order pattern with the instinctual physical impulse, falls apart; it is only then, as Jung points out,[30] that there is a split and the religious teaching begins to be hostile and poisonous to instinctual physical impulsiveness. Such splits as we face here in Dorn, and which we meet to a tremendous extent throughout the whole history of Christianity, have occurred before in many other religions and have probably been occasioned by the unconscious itself in order to increase consciousness.

We know that ultimately all conflicts are created not only by, let us say, a wrong conscious attitude, but by the unconscious itself, in order to reunite the opposites on a higher level. Therefore the situation in which a religious doctrine or teaching or tradition is poisonous and destructive to the physical instinctuality of man is to be viewed not only as a catastrophe or a deviation from the original pattern, but just as much a provocation of the unconscious psyche to bring forth higher consciousness. If this goes too far, however, then one gets into a split situation and experiences such a tension of opposites that one completely loses his inner balance and even his capacity for survival. In such cases, when the unconscious has, so to speak, created the split, it afterwards also produces symbols that are meant to reconcile it. The most frequent symbols that occur in such a moment are those of a great healer or a God-man or savior figure who again unites the opposites, overcomes the split, and brings a new order of things in which the physical instinctuality of man, his original roots, so to speak, and his unconscious come together again in living cooperation, as a new vision or a new order of things.

Originally, therefore (and Dorn even recognizes this later), one could assume that nobody is less greedy or unbalanced than animals and primitive man. Instinct in its original form carries its own measure in itself. Animals very rarely overeat—perhaps dogs do, and then vomit, but that is generally because they have already entered the disturbed areas of man. People have interfered with dogs' feeding habits and rhythms, so let us not take domestic animals as an example; they have all been ruined by our influence. But animals that live in pure nature never overdo anything, neither sex nor food nor anything else, because their patterns of behavior always determine the right measure and the moment to stop. The moment to start and the moment to stop are both built into their behavioral system, which is why Jung always said that animals were much more pious and religious than people, because they really obey their inner order and really follow the meaning of what they are meant to be, never going beyond that. It is only man who is able to do that, and we know to what extent.

You see, the body says something very interesting here, namely: *mens* mind is associated in Latin with *mensa* (table), *mensura* (measure), and *mensis* (month; plural, *menses*). Thus he suddenly has a correct intuition and says, "Oh, we are relations. You are the *mens*—that means the one who wants to concentrate on the spiritual order; but what I am interested

in is life here on this earth, eating and such things; there is
*mens* in that too." If the *corpus* had been allowed to talk a little
more, they could have shaken hands and agreed that basically
they were following the same line. The body should listen to
its own *mensura* of the *mensa*, and that is exactly what the *mens*
wants, so there need be no conflict. But the *mens,* having its
emotional prejudices, just goes on: "Oh, you should not have
eaten like that, you should remember that you are going to
die soon," and goes off into an emotional sermon to the poor
body.

Therefore, one has to read the text very carefully. If you
do that and always remember to listen to what the body says,
then you realize that there would have been a possibility of
union. But the *mens,* just to intimidate the body, brandishes
the threat of death, and naturally he does not like that. Even
then, though, the body is quite understanding in a way, or is
really willing to understand, because he then says, "Well, tell
me, what is death?" And then come all these rather conventional phrases like, "You come from death and therefore will
return to death," and "The *anima* is in between [life and
death] but she will be saved in eternity," and "You, the body,
are just afraid of death." Then the poor body says, "Well, I
am no wiser than I was before."

So, in spite of his attempt to understand, the body cannot
get along with what the *mens* has in mind. It looks as if they
just accuse each other of being crazy and cannot unite. As you
will see later on, it is not as bad as it looks at this point in the
discussion. Mens then continues to try to explain a litte about
death.

MENS: Listen, what you call death, to me stands for the beginning of eternal life, and I cannot imagine anything more
agreeable, but you hate death because it takes you away from
wordly pleasures. You should know that between worldly
pleasures and eternal pleasure there is a relationship like that
between gall and honey, but you know yourself that all pleasure [the *mens* means unmeasured pleasure—*lust* is a negative

word; in Latin it is *voluptas*, which, as you know, means eating
too much and overdoing things] ends in nausea, and after the
nausea come even worse things: illness and finally death.
When you eat, you always want more and more, and you
never stop wanting more, and with drinking it's the same, and
in spite of that you are afraid of death. Yet you bring about
your own death, you insatiable body. He who cannot protect
himself against what is bad for him, and who is afraid of what
he himself is, is the human body who does not live in the
harmony of the *mens* [you see, the *mens* claims to have the
right measure], and he is more unhappier than all the animals
because the animals only want what is absolutely necessary
for them.

In a secret way the *mens* returns to what the body wanted
to say. She has now really accepted that wisdom and knows
that the animals have no such problem and that if the human
body, as far it is an animal, only listened to its inner nausea
and other reactions, which are the reactions that give us a
hint of inner measure, then there would be no problem. So
with a detour, and while pretending not to agree, the *mens*
now preaches what the body was driving at before, so they
are not really as far apart as it looks. It's only man with his
reason who can overdo things and even eat what kills him.
But then there comes a long, moralistic sermon against
overvaluing the pleasures of the body: "Oh, poor body, you
are really only afraid of yourself, because from you comes
death through desirousness." What really happens is that the
*mens* accuses the body of being wrong not in himself—he is
O.K., really, in himself, Mens admits that—but because he has
this unmeasured desirousness. From a modern standpoint we
would say that exaggerated desirousness was a psychological
problem and has nothing to do with the body, but is connected with the shadow.
*So the* mens *projected the shadow onto the body* and then gave
him all those sermons, but if we separate the shadow from
the body and take the latter for what he is—namely, a quite

reasonable animal that has its own inner spiritual laws—
without accusing him and saying that this desirousness comes
from him, then the discussion could have been on another
level, and the question put as to where that measureless desirousness came from. Where did this neurotic tendency to
overeat and so forth come into the picture? Nowadays we
would see it clearly as a psychological problem and not blame
the body, but at that time, lacking the concept of the unconscious, people could not understand it that way.

Then the *mens* continues to project, saying: They have
an unclarified shadow problem, which they just throw at one
another, each accusing the other of inconsistency. The *mens*,
however, is not logical at all but skips around in her logic,
saying:

> Now, see how inconsistent you are; you cannot resist
> other people or even yourself. Now please be as reason-
> able as possible and do not hesitate so much, because
> we have to run to the gardens of Frequentia [that is,
> repetition] and there you will hear more about it!

Then a short passage recapitulates the fourth chapter,
which describes the third degree of inner development:

> You must know, brothers, that everything I have men-
> tioned before, and everything I am going to mention
> afterwards, can be referred to the alchemical prepara-
> tion. What I have said about the parts of man as a sepa-
> ration through speculative philosophy can just as well
> be applied to a separation of one element from all the
> other bodies.

Dorn suddenly was afraid that one could misunderstand
this as a purely inner moral discussion, as a kind of moral
problem, as somebody discussing his own drives within himself, and not understand it as an explanation of *real* alchemy,
*real* chemistry. In this early stage of chemistry the simplest

way to separate the different substances was to heat them up. As you know, all the different elements have a different degree at which they begin to evaporate, so if you have a lot of chemicals and you heat them up, first one element leaves and you can precipitate it, and then another and you can precipitate again, and so on. And at that time they frequently separated the different chemical elements and alloys like that The *mens* says here that with heat you can separate different substances,

> and that is what I am doing in this dialogue. I am really using a fire to separate all the different elements. Therefore it is not to be understood as a moralistic religious sermon like a text by a medieval saint, but should be understood chemically, and if such a separation is not done, then the alchemists will never find the universal medicine to cure all illness. There is not one word in this whole book that does not refer to the art of alchemy and its explanation.

Thus Dorn wants to ward off the idea, which one easily might get, that he only means an inner mental conflict of man and not an event in nature. You see here how again the concept of the collective unconscious, as Jung conceived it, serves as a saving factor. Only through that concept can we see an inner conflict objectively, without projecting it either onto the body or onto the subject.

The *mens* is more or less a well-meaning developed ego consciousness, with religious conviction and self-control, having at its disposition the whole wisdom of the Christian tradition, while the body carries the projection of a whole lot of things which we now would call the unconscious, and more specifically, the shadow.

But lacking the concept of the unconscious, Dorn could not solve this problem: either this conflict is in the *mens*, and then the tension is at the ego level, or it is a purely chemical disturbance in nature. Among modern people, eighty percent still think that way, because they have not yet even seen the importance of the concept of the unconscious. They still see only a subject with personal conflicts, and the *mens* is naturally in the same position. There has always been a tendency to misunderstand the conflicts either materialistically— thinking that the whole problem is in the body, which has to be cured by chemical medicine—or psychologically, but with the implication that the problem lies simply in what the subject thinks about itself, the complications the ego has with and makes for itself. The idea that the conflict could lie in another realm, that is, in the unconscious psyche where the cure lies also, naturally did not exist. You will now understand why Jung had to go back to the seventeenth century and be imprisoned in it and pick up the process from there.[31]

But here Dorn clearly asserts (for he has gradually realized it) that he is talking not just about a conscious conflict, but about something else: a healing factor—he would say, a divine spiritual healing factor in matter or in nature. And that is why he ends this chapter by saying one should understand what he writes not as a moral conflict, but as an alchemical procedure.

Dorn goes on to explain that even further:

> The Philosophical love and the enmity within the material part is just the same as in the parts of man. The union of the two can only be achieved if one first removes the corruption before the *coniunctio*, which is why one must make peace between the enemies so that they can become friends. In all imperfect bodies [metals as you find them in nature] which have not yet achieved their complete perfection, there is a state of friendship and enmity at the same time. But if, with great understanding and effort, man removes the enmity, then, as we explained, they achieve perfection through becoming one in man. Therefore, separate the impure parts in each body by fire and purify them (the pure parts do not need that). Then mix again what has been purified with the

pure, and what is heavy with what is light, and after you have sublimated that, then you can make what is fixed, volatile, and what is physical, spiritual.

You see how Dorn proceeds: he starts with religious teaching, then he goes down into the problem as it is in man with his conflicts, then he applies it to the body, and then to the general elements in nature, and there he says that in outer nature—let us say in a bit of ore or in a bit of wood or stone—there is exactly the same situation as with man: that is, a state of hostile tension, of enmity on one side and a certain amount of love on the other. He means repulsion and affinity in a physical sense, and there too you have to proceed by removing the repulsion, or the enmity, of all the different parts, so that they can all be united.

His association with the history of alchemy would be that the gold, now really understood as a metal, is the perfect state of every metal. Iron, copper, and alloy, and so forth, are just not—yet—completed metals, hampered by stuff which is inimical to them. Therefore, if you make this higher *separatio* and remove what hampers the inner development of that metal, it will naturally become gold.

That was the alchemists' theory, and we are not yet so convinced that this can really be applied in this coarse way, at least not to matter. To us, however, it is a clear representation of what we discover in the unconscious, which contains conflicting and disintegrating tendencies at the same time. The disintegrating tendencies may result in psychosis if the unconscious and consciousness clash, for then the conflict has prevailed and the person falls into all those parts which are hostile to each other, as, for instance, when the psychotic person hears different voices that quarrel with each other. On the other hand, we also know that the unconscious contains synthesizing or integrating tendencies, which issue from that regulating center which Jung calls the Self.

The Self is the center of integrating tendencies and of healing within the unconscious, so we can say that in that way we still proceed exactly like the alchemists. We try to remove the enmity between the elements, not by discarding it, but by forcing people to have it out with their own conflicts, to confront themselves with their own conflicts instead of just letting them happen in the unconscious, and by supporting the integrating tendency of the unconscious. If somebody has dreams that propose a solution, we proceed by making those dreams and their tendencies rise into consciousness and supporting and encouraging, so to speak, the integrating tendencies. Very often in such dream motifs one sees the enmity of the elements as animals fighting: as in many fairy tales and myths, a bird and a snake fight, or two birds, or two dogs are locked together in a fight.[32] Fighting animals always refer to a conflict within the unconscious itself, when two instinctual tendencies within the unconscious lock horns. If consciousness steps in, then the conflict changes.

The same thing happens in fairy tales where the hero finds animals fighting and makes peace between them and then gets gifts from them. One gives him an eagle's feather and says, "Whenever you call me, I will help you," and the other gives him a hair from its tail and says, "Whenever you are in need, just take the hair and burn it and I will come to your help."[33] That is a motif in innumerable myths and fairy tales. There too is this enmity of different elements within the unconscious, which through the interference of consciousness can be solved by a compromise or by making the conflict conscious. That clears the way so that the integrating tendencies of the Self can come through and work for the integration and unification of the personality. These conflicts issue partly from environmental influence and probably also from the fact that in our psyche we inherit conflicting tendencies from our forefathers. We are generally born with a certain number of these, and if we do not attend to them, they war within us, fight among themselves behind our back, and so weaken and distract the conscious personality. These conflicts can be observed on an animal level: who has never seen a little dog

move backward while furiously barking, trembling and fearful
of a big dog?

Dorn continues:

> I must now admonish the reader to make certain dis-
> tinctions so that he does not become confused and begin
> through that to doubt the whole thing. If I mention
> soulless things, I am referring to the vegetative and
> mineral kingdoms, that is, to the plant and stone and
> metal kingdoms of earth. Those things, however, also
> have their vegetative and mineral souls. Therefore, if I
> speak of dead bodies, nobody should think that I want
> to go against alchemists who believe that everything in
> nature has a spirit, a soul, and a body.

Dorn thinks that even what we coarsely call dead matter has
a kind of psyche of its own, though of a different quality than
the human psyche. When he speaks of dead matter, he is
speaking colloquially; he is convinced that there is no such
thing as dead matter. Dorn grants the animal a soul, not a
rational one but a sensitive soul, endowed with, we would say,
a more vague ego consciousness.

*Sensitiva* here means capable of sense, of affections and
feelings. Some behaviorists still think in the Cartesian way
that animals are pure physical automata. But more and more,
certain schools are coming to the conclusion that animals do
indeed have the rudimentary beginnings of all the psychic
qualities that we have, though perhaps not so developed, and
that the higher mammals have feelings and reactions very
similar to ours. That is why the ethologist Konrad Lorenz
said as a joke that animals are people of the feeling type. Anybody who knows them would agree with that, and Dorn
seems to have a similar idea.

> One has to understand what I explained before, that
> there is a double rational separation [rational = *ratio*:
> having the right vision of things]: one is the voluntary

separation which I discussed before, and the other is the
natural separation, which does not belong to alchemy.
[By that he means natural death.] In death the same
thing happens, but that does not belong to alchemy; that
is just an event. But the separation of the perceiving soul
and the so-called dead body is also double, for again one
is natural and the other artificial, and again only the
latter belongs to alchemy. The voluntary separation
happens in a state in which all parts remain preserved,
which does not happen in the natural separation. In
death the body is destroyed, but if I anticipate the experience of death, as I do here in this alchemical procedure,
then the body is preserved and it is separated, put aside,
and preserved, and I can pick it up again later. But if
that same separation happens through the body, I cannot pick up the body again; it is destroyed. The instrument of voluntary separation is the spirit and the breath
of life, and the instrument of natural separation is death,
and the instrument of artificial separation [i.e., in the
retort] is fire. But I would not object if one put into one
the alchemy of the *rationalia* [by that he means what
he described before in the dialogue] with the effective
sensation and so-called dead body.

That sounds very strange, because Dorn always talks of them
as two, but says he would not object if one understood them
as one. In other words, he is just not capable of using what
one could call a unitarian language and so is always forced to
talk about so-called outer things in the retort or in the metal,
and so-called inner psychic facts, which he calls *rationalia* and
we would call the unconscious. But he claims to have no ob-
jection if you really understand them as one.

Dorn is up against a difficulty that we still have in modern
psychology. The physicist Wolfgang Pauli always said that
we should now proceed to find a neutral, or unitarian, language in which every concept we use is applicable to the unconscious as well as to matter, in order to overcome this false

view that the unconscious psyche and matter are two things.³⁴
We still do not yet have this unitarian language to any extent,
and Dorn had it even less. Thus he was forced to speak in a
dual way, yet at the same time he always assures us that it
must be understood somehow as one. He cannot get beyond
that because he is hampered by the language of his time in
expressing his intuition of unity. But he says here: "I do not
want to evoke the appearance of having left natural alchemy."
Anyone who reads this exceedingly moral, ethical quarrel
could say, "Well, that is a moral and theological problem.
What does that have to do with natural alchemy?"—meaning
what happens in the retort—but Dorn does not want to give
that impression.

He continues:

> One has to understand it in the right way, and I there-
> fore will now begin with the *separatio*. You know that
> man only lives for a certain time, and then in accordance
> with nature he is dissolved into spirit, soul, and body,
> and the body is dissolved in putrefaction in death. Then
> the natural fire in the body, the warmth of the body,
> stops and the *humor radicalis*, the basic radical moisture
> of the body, stops flowing. Then the spirit and the soul
> leave the body and the body is put into the earth, and
> there, through the process of putrefaction it disinte-
> grates into its elementary parts, each one returning to
> its element: the earth devours the earthly parts of the
> body, the water the liquid, and so on. Spirit and soul,
> however, return to their origin, but they should not re-
> main separated from their body forever and therefore
> are reunited with it in a better composition later on
> through a divine artifice, so that afterwards they will no
> longer be separated. And the highest value of the union
> lies in the fact that they become an inseparable melting
> together of all parts into one.

Here Dorn describes the idea of the glorified body, or of the
physical resurrection after death, as it is taught in Christian-

ity. To him natural death is interpreted as a temporary separation during which the body is disintegrated and the other two parts are separated. Then God is the great alchemist who afterwards, through divine artifice, reunites them. He somehow makes the body resurrect, and then, in that second union of body, mind, and soul, they really become completely one.

You will remember what I told you before, that one of the roots of alchemy derived from the Egyptian endeavor to create an eternal body. Many chemical and alchemical procedures are actual continuations of the Egyptians' chemical attempts to mummify the body so as to create an eternal body as support and goal for the continuation of spirit and soul after death. Thus you see how much this archetype goes through the centuries.

Dorn takes the Christian teaching of the glorified body in the same way as the Egyptians, for whom the actual mummy was what we would now call the glorified body, a chemically transformed body, whereas for Christians the idea is that God performs that miracle. You have probably seen those medieval pictures where half-distintegrated skeletons come out of their graves when the angel blows the last trumpet, and then there are all those awful problems as to whether you will be as ugly as you were on earth, and what happens if somebody has lost a leg? Will that person be reborn with a wooden leg?

This problem of the glorified body has therefore always been a great stumbling block for believers. Even today, if you ask a parson how that will happen, he will be very embarrassed to answer. Dorn's faith was intact. He believed in the Christian doctrine and was convinced of it. And now we are getting on the right track, for if God can do that, then the alchemist, if he could get into contact with God's creative spirit, could do it too, and could even do it during in his lifetime! Naturally he cannot do it just through his own strength, but through meditation he could contact God, who has the secret of how to create an eternal body. That way you could, while still living, create within yourself by psychological efforts an immortal or glorified body, before natural death.

That is the whole opus, and there Dorn, along with many other alchemists, reaches a viewpoint that is completely familiar to the East and to certain Christian mystics.

In certain Yoga exercises for creating the diamond body and in those described in *The Secret of the Golden Flower*,[35] which is a kind of Chinese Yoga meditation text, the purpose is to create within the mortal body a kind of subtle body, the abode of the spirit and the soul after death. Then, when disintegration takes place, the actually dying body is cast off like a shell, and out comes that immortal glorified body that has already been created inwardly through psychological effort and meditation. Thus an idea which is completely familiar to the East occurs in the West practically only in alchemy, because the alchemists were sufficiently concerned about the body and the problem of its glorification.

# 5

### ❈

# MEDIEVAL MAGIC AND MODERN SYNCHRONICITY

WE LEFT OFF IN THE MIDDLE of the degree of *Potentia,* or power, sometimes also called *Frequentia,* meaning endurance or perseverance. Our heroes have come to the castle of Frequentia, who has given the *mens* and the body a long sermon about how the work in the garden of the opus should be begun, namely, in a kind of long, enduring, patient, regular exercise of the realization that they had had before.

The image of the gardener appears very often in alchemy, and the head gardener in older texts is generally the god Saturn, mixed up as always in the Middle Ages with the idea of the planet Saturn. There are many old woodcuts in alchemical texts where Saturn, like an old gardener with a wooden leg, goes around and attends the garden of the so-called sun and moon plant, where the sun and moon plant, or the sun and moon trees, grow. So, in medieval associations, Saturn means a kind of resigned, melancholy, exceedingly introverted, even closed-in attitude, cut off from all outer activities, even from feeling, and with a closeness to the coldness of death and depression.

Here it is not Saturn but Frequentia—endurance or perseverance—who does the job. She gives a slightly more optimistic tinge to the whole thing but is still very much associated with these former ideas. We come promptly to the idea of an inner death in the next part as well:

> Now irrigate your body with the water of life, i.e., with the word of God. Day and night meditate about it, so that the body has no time to talk or think of anything else. The good earth is a soft heart which is ashamed and humble. Since the fall of Adam, the hearts of men have become hard as stones, and if they are not softened again by the word of God, they will remain stones forever, and so we all become enemies of God till this enmity is again overcome through the highest gardener and his servant, the *mens*. Therefore let us thank God, who thought us worthy to enlighten our hearts with His light and soften it with His word. Go now and try to find the virtue.

This is a stage in alchemy that alludes to a so-called second death and then to the *multiplicatio*, and also to the *proiectio*. Again, please do not associate Jungian terminology with that. In general, it is the stage where the philosopher's stone, after it has been made in the retort, has to be destroyed again several times and then remade, a kind of complete repetition of the work, which generally is done four times. This repeated destruction of the philosopher's stone and its remaking was called the *rotatio*, a rotation through the four elements. After that the retort is usually broken or opened, and then begins the stage of the *multiplicatio* through projection.

The idea is that the philosopher's stone, which is also a form of the mystical gold that the alchemists were trying to make, is made and is then thrown upon other, unclean matter—that is, other matter which has not been included in the process, like ordinary iron, ordinary lead, or any other material. It shows then a transformative quality, for it transforms these other materials through *proiectio*, projection. It transforms them into gold and has what one could call a positive, contagious effect on other materials. If, as an alchemist, you have made one bit of material of this mystical gold in the retort, then, when you open it, it emanates onto other material. Sometimes that is varied by the idea that you have not made solid but liquid or drinkable gold, or a kind of elixir, and then the *proiectio* multiplication corresponds to the healing afterwards for other people and other things. It has again this kind of emanating positive contagious effect.

This stage is also to be found in certain exercises of Eastern meditation, particularly in Zen Buddhism. After you have found *samadhi*—inner illumination or, we would say, contact with or an experience of the Self—there comes the problem of how to go on in life. Therefore, in the famous series of Zen Buddhist Oxherding Pictures,[36] after the novice has had the great experience of transcendence and illumination, or *samadhi*, there is a last picture where a wise old man with a kind of insipid, friendly smile on his face walks with a begging bowl accompanied by his *chela* (student), and the poem runs: "He has forgotten the gods, he has even forgotten his enlightenment. Quite simply he goes to the marketplace begging, but wherever he goes, the cherry trees blossom."

There you see the healing effect on outer things, even on nature. It is a return to a naive, unconscious way of living, which also means living naively again within reality as it is, without any artificial effort to hold back emotion, fantasy, or thought, but rather keeping it in the retort and so seemingly returning to the initial stage of unconsciousness. Naturally this is not really the case, for it is on a higher level, which manifests indirectly in the fact that the Zen master at this stage has reached softness of heart and a capacity to live in the way that perhaps has been best described by Lao-tzu: the softness and the sadness in which he feels he is alone while all other people think they know everything, know what they want, and what they think.[37] Here in the alchemical *multiplicatio*, though projected onto matter, is the same idea: namely, the *mulitiplicatio* as a return to the initial stage, a breaking of the retort, which would mean stopping the artificial exercise of introversion and of introjecting one's own projections, thus allowing the unconscious to flow through oneself without constantly concentrating on it—an absolute reversal of the beginning stage of what we do.

For instance, in analysis, when people project onto the outer world, or give in to their feelings and affects naively, we try to make them take the projections back and see the thing objectively as an inner factor. That very exercise is now reversed, and the unconscious is allowed to flow through the person and then have a positive effect upon the surroundings. Dorn, who was basically Christian, compares this to a softening of the heart and preparation to receive the Word of God, which would mean a feeling-realization of the Christian truth.

Dorn amplifies this problem of the heart in his famous commentary on a paper by Paracelsus entitled "De vita longa," on which Jung has made a very extended commentary in his longer paper on Paracelsus. The essence of the teaching represented there comes from Paracelsus, but Dorn has added very enlightening amplifications. The associations that Dorn probably had in mind are as follows: the heart, according to Paracelsus and Dorn, is the seat of excitement, of emotion and feeling, of the feeling life; it is therefore a very restless thing. It is very easily affected and is constantly moved negatively or positively by outer and inner experiences. It thereby uses itself up, which most frequently leads to a premature death through some circulatory or heart disease. Therefore one could say that if people use themselves up prematurely, this has very often to do with too much uncontrolled feeling and emotion, leading to the "manager's disease" or heart attack.

The heart has, roughly speaking, a quaternarian structure, or at least Paracelsus and Dorn saw it in this form. Therefore, to the medical philosophers of that time, it was a symbol of the Self, but as a feeling-realization. They assumed that in the heart there was a certain amount of air, which tended to break through and cause sudden death or a heart attack. Thus the meditative exercise they proposed was to let that air out of the heart and to diminish emotional or feeling-reactions toward outer events, so as to react completely to the rhythms of the Self. In very complicated alchemical language there is an effort in that paper to explain a reconditioning of the heart by which it would become quiet and have a regular, quiet rhythm; it would still have feeling-reactions, but only those directed toward what Paracelsus and Dorn describe as the *Adech* or *Aniadus* and other such complicated names.

Jung has unraveled this secret language and shown that what these authors meant with these names corresponds to what we now would call the Self. For instance, *Adech* is the eternal man and has such associations. This reconditioning of the heart prolongs people's lives. That was the medical theory of Paracelsus and Dorn, and I can only say that I think, look-ing at it from a modern standpoint, that there is quite a lot to it. In our context, making the heart soft and no longer rebel-lious alludes to similar associations, namely that the heart has not this kind of autonomous dependence on the ego, on ego desires and impulses, but becomes peaceful and detached. The feeling function, being detached from outer things, then opens toward the Word of God and to a kind of feeling-realization of the Christian doctrine. That is the essence of this gardening process and is the answer to the last sentence which I quoted before in the text where Dorn has the *mens* say that you have to weed out all evil thoughts, enmity, and evil deeds; but then Dorn makes a sudden strange leap of thought: he adds that evil deeds and thoughts are conceived not by the body, but by the *animus* through the secret exercise of his imagination, which the body puts into effect.

I pointed out in the previous chapter that a sudden tre-mendous turn has taken place, for until now we always had the idea that the body was the seat of evil and of all those measureless appetites, and that the *mens* was the reasonable and higher part of the personality that has to subdue and edu-cate this rebellious body. In other words, what we call the shadow was projected onto the physical man, and then sud-denly we hear that the body does not conceive any evil, it is completely all right and innocent, but that there are secret exercises of evil imagination which obviously come from the person who conceives evil and then makes the body carry it out. One could say that now the shadow projection onto the body has been taken back; the latter has returned to its original innocence, and the author realizes that the problem of evil is now within the *mens*, within that part of the personality which before was described as being pure and in accordance with the Christian doctrine. The idea now arises that the seat of evil is the heart.

In summing up the development of Dorn's thought, we see that leaving the body aside, *animus* and *anima* together made *mens*. The main part of the active imagination I quoted concerned the discussion between *mens* and *corpus*; the latter, who has lost *anima*, wedded to the *mens*, does not want to join her. *Mens* preaches to *corpus*, and they project onto each other and call each other crazy.

But owing to a sudden shift, Dorn for the first time includes evil in the exercises of the *animus*. Evil is taken back into the light and more conscious part of the partner, but then it is again projected, this time into the heart.[38] The next question would really be to ask where that evil comes from which the *animus* possesses in its secret exercises of imagination. But is the heart into which evil is now projected meant as a physical or psychological organ? Here again Dorn speaks ambiguously. So the heart is conceived of as a new object onto which to project the battle, and is in position in between matter and spirit, between a spiritual and a material entity; it is this in-between zone where the psychological conflict is now carried on. There is still, however, this Christian idea that evil has to be absolutely thrown out and cannot be integrated; it has to be thrown out of the heart, which means that the hardening of the heart and its emotionality and rebellious reactions have somehow to be reeducated. This process has happened again and again in the development of science in recent times: the unconscious psyche has always been projected onto some other part of the body. For Descartes, for instance, it was the pineal gland.[39] Later the brain myth ap-

peared, which still holds good for a number of modern neu-
rologists, psychiatrists, and psychologists, who project the
unconscious onto the brain. In this way the projection slowly
moves on. The most primitive tribes generally project the
psyche into the fat of the kidneys—for instance, the Austra-
lian aborigines, certain African tribes project it onto the belly,
and for the North American Indians the seat of the psyche is
the heart,[40] which would be the same stage as here. Later on
it went, as mentioned, into the pineal gland and afterwards
into the brain.

Thus the projection always falls onto a part of the body.
In this passage of our text, after an aborted attempt to bring
more clarity into the problem of evil by making the *mens* (or
rather its *animus*) responsible, the projection restarts and everything again becomes vague. The body soon will catch up
with that, but it is a bit slow and has not got to the point
immediately. So Mens goes on preaching that in every kind
of art, and naturally, therefore, also in the art of alchemy, one
needs what one could call a regular exercise of self-education;
that is why Mens adds that few people have succeeded in producing the universal medicine: first those, who through the
grace of God had transformed themselves into what they
were looking for. That means that before you can find the
universal medicine you desire to reach in this *opus*, you must
first become it yourself.

The text continues:

> They cleansed their bodies from all impurity and they
> removed the cloud from the natural body. Therefore I
> advise you, students of this great art, first to pray to
> God and then to study and work, and perhaps then it
> will happen to you that you reach what the giver of light
> can give you in the name of Christ; but first reflect well
> what it means to ask the Father in the Son.

There is one concept here that refers to a long historical past
of symbology, namely, the concept of the cloud. In alchemy,

the symbol of the cloud plays an enormous role, because the word *cloud* was used for any kind of sublimated or evaporated substance. When you evaporate a material in a retort, then naturally the upper part of the retort gets cloudy and one sees vapors, and that is what the alchemist compared to the clouds in the sky. The image of the cloud also had a mystical sense. We know, for instance, the medieval mystical text *The Cloud of Unknowing*, written in monastic circles by an unknown author. This text contains a series of spiritual exercises to prepare the adept for such an experience.

The cloud within the world of Christian mysticism implied that as one got closer and closer to the divine light through meditation, spiritual exercises, humility, and docility, ultimately the light of God appeared, not as a big illumination, but as a darkening of the human light and an experience of darkness and confusion. On the other hand, in medieval language the cloud was also always associated with the mental confusion caused by the devil. Many such texts are quoted in *Aion*.[41] Jung has compiled a collection that describes the North Pole as a seat of constant lack of sun and cloudiness. In this nebula, in the mist and clouds dwells the devil, who from there blows his confusing unconsciousness over the whole world. So you see, the cloud is what surrounds the devil and God—in other words, what surrounds the symbol of the Self in its light and dark aspect.[42] In practice it corresponds to an experience that people do not like to accept, but to which Jung has again and again referred: namely, that with increasing progress in the process of individuation, the deeper and closer people get to the Self within themselves, the more confused and complicated the situation becomes. It does not become easier.

We often asked Jung whether the process of individuation was most difficult in the beginning or at the end, and he said it was difficult at both. In the beginning the difficulty lies in one's unconsciousness about one's shadow and animus or anima, and most people know how one can be tortured and confused by these problems, but this form of confusion usually slowly subsides. The infantile stupidity with which most human beings torture themselves in the beginning of the process slowly fades away. In that way the beginning is most difficult, and then things become easier. Once one has really discovered that there is no progress and no solution other than getting used to that very simple thing of again and again just looking in every situation at the subjective factor of all the disturbances and trying to integrate it on that level—then a lot of the outer difficulties and the nonsense with which one was tortured just fall away. Thus one could hope that the process of individuation, in the course of its development, though terrible at the beginning, would get lighter and more satisfactory, comparable to what occurs with the spiritual exercise and the symbolism of alchemy, which partly promise the same thing. The alchemical progression, the *nigredo, albedo, rubedo,* and *citrinatis,* inspires hope that better and higher states of the inner situation may be reached.

This is not, however, the whole truth, though one cannot explain why it is so; in practice one sees that the longer people work on this road, the more subtle the indications of the unconscious become and the worse one gets punished or thrown off if one makes a slight mistake. In the beginning stages, people can commit the most horrible sins of unconsciousness and stupidity without having to pay much for it. Nature does not take revenge. But when the work progresses over the years, even a slight deviation, a hint of the wrong word, or a fleeting wrong thought can have the worst psychosomatic consequences. It is as though it became ever more subtle, moving on the razor's edge. Any faux pas is an abysmal catastrophe, while previously one could plod kilometers off the path without one's own unconscious giving one a slap or taking its revenge in any way.

This is naturally an increasing difficulty, and with it goes the fact that people in a later stage of the analytical process have dreams that are more difficult to interpret. In the beginning stage what the dreams say to people is obvious. The people themselves perhaps cannot see it, but for the analyst it entails no effort, it just lies there visibly on the table. But the longer the process continues, the more the dreams become seemingly confused or paradoxical, or subtle and very complicated. Also the problems, if one should interpret them on the subjective or objective level, become much more subtle. For instance, people who have gone a long way on this path dream more frequently about objective outer situations. It is as if they had cleaned their own psyches: that does not bother them anymore, their own shadow problems are cleaned up, so to speak. Then certain problems in the world or the world situation or problems of the objective surroundings become more imminent or urgent. Whereas in the beginning it is generally not advisable to take dreams on the objective level, the more the process proceeds, the more other problems come into question. This makes it very difficult, because whether to interpret a dream on the subjective or objective level is a feeling decision.

We have not yet found any valid scientific criterion for deciding whether a dream points to some outer situation that we do no know yet—whether it is a prognostication, for instance, of future events, which do not concern the personal inner situation—or whether it should be taken as an inner drama, as we normally and habitually do. The closer one comes to the Self, the more dangerous the situation becomes and the more one gets into a cloud of confusion. So the cloud, or the removal of the cloud, has to do with an effort to penetrate this confused situation.

In our text the cloud obviously has first to be removed from the natural body, and that would refer to unconsciousness at the beginning stage. In modern language, we would now interpret it as the taking back of projections. But as I said, this cloud does not then disappear, it only moves into another realm, and you will see that the *mens* promptly gets completely lost in that cloud.

We come to a little bit of active imagination in the form of a further dialogue. It is the dialogue in which the *mens* and the body discourse with each other.

MENS: Have you heard what Frequentia said?

BODY: Yes.

MENS: Do you like it?

BODY: Not 'specially.

MENS: Why not?

BODY: Well, this is all very complicated, but I do not know what it is aiming at.

MENS: Well, to your own happiness.

BODY: Well, I hope so.

MENS: Tell me, do you know that there is a second life after this one?

BODY: Yes, I know.

MENS: And that there is also an eternal death?

BODY: I know that too.

MENS: Therefore you should live in this world as if you lived forever.

BODY: Well, I try to, as you see.

MENS: No, on the contrary, from day to day you die more and more.

BODY: You're crazy.

MENS: Now, listen, the people who live in this world die *with* the world, and only those who live in Christ die *for* the world.

BODY: Who can understand that?

MENS: Haven't you read in the Gospels that if the corn does not fall onto the earth and die, it remains alone?

BODY: What has that to do with the whole thing?

MENS: You are the corn that has fallen onto the earth, because you consist of earth.

BODY: Oh, but I just heard Frequentia say that the corn was the Word of God.

MENS: Well, I notice that you have listened.

BODY: Naturally.

MENS: You are not a good theologian.

BODY: Please explain.

MENS: If the word, the simile of the corn, is referred to the Word of God, then it has an active meaning: namely, the Word of God falls into the human heart and dies there; but one can also understand it in the passive sense, that unless the body and the human heart which have been sown on the ground (i.e., have become earthly), are killed and then receive the corn of the Word of God, they cannot be transformed and bear fruit. Or, to put it in a more Christian sense, if the corn of the Word of God is not united with the dead body, then both remain separate and without fruit.

BODY: Now you're even bringing grammar into it [active and passive verbs].

MENS: You are still rebellious, Body, and I must keep you on the path of virtue, but now we have reached another place.

Here the discussion falls completely apart and they just talk illogically. Mens becomes full of theological sophistications, and the body very correctly points that out, and Mens does not answer except by scolding. They are at cross purposes, both completely in the clouds or confused. So they wobble on without any solution for the time being, and they knock at the castle of Virtus, which is the fifth philosophical degree.

*Virtus* is the same word as the English word *virtue*, but in the sixteenth century it did not yet completely have that meaning. The root is *vir*, man. *Virtus*, therefore, in the language of the sixteenth century, has to do with male activity, efficiency, and effectiveness, so to speak. One also spoke about the *virtus* of a chemical substance, and then it meant its active effects. If a substance has the *virtus* of doing this or that, that means it has an active effect upon other chemical things. We have to understand *virtus* in this connotation.

Here is the discussion in brief:

MENS: Please open your holy doors.

VIRTUS: Who is it? Who are you?

MENS: Two pupils of philosophy.

VIRTUS: What do you want?

MENS: To learn virtue.

VIRTUS: That is a good thing that cannot be refused, but who was your former teacher?

MENS: Love of Philosophy and Frequentia.

VIRTUS: I am glad you began there. Why have you started on these studies?

MENS: To find truth.

VIRTUS: That is the root and mother of everything that God created, the discovery of truth. But what do you want now?

MENS: We want to practice it.

VIRTUS: Towards whom?

MENS: Towards God and our neighbor.

VIRTUS: That is a good intention, and I hope God will let you succeed. What is your name?

MENS: I am called Mens, and this fellow here is Body.

VIRTUS: How did you get these names?

MENS: I got my name from Philosophical Love but Body is just called *vulgo* that way.

BODY: What has Mens to do with Body?

MENS: Nothing, we are in conflict on every point.

BODY: What do I hear?

VIRTUS: Body does not want to leave the world. Everything that has fallen into the world flees from salvation and can only be brought back with the greatest effort. But please come in, brethren, and I shall see what I can do for you. Sit down, Body, and eat and drink; I will feed Mens separately.

Then follows another prayer by Virtus that God may aid the work, after which Virtus adds a polemic against the split between theology and *virtus*: in other words, against intellectual theorizing that would separate the image of God from *virtus*, the latter being ethical obligations and behavior. He insists that the truth of what one thinks, and the truth of how one acts, must remain one, arguing against the well-known split that the intellect thinks one thing while the ethical and moral obligations are written down and put into another drawer.

To us that is more or less a self-evident problem, which therefore does not deviate from what any modern Christian writer could say. We all know that most people, or very many people, have a compartmentalized psychology: when they write a paper or read books, or, for instance, when clergy preach, they turn on one part of their personality, and when it comes to behavior at home or in their practical life, they turn on another. Most people have these compartments unconsciously. If one tried to pin them down by quoting what they said five minutes before, then they just start to fib or to fidget or get irritable. Confronting people with their compartmental psychology in analysis generally does not happen without a huge emotional explosion. These compartments are watertight and cut off, and if you try to open the door between them, there is generally terrific confusion and a desperate struggle of the person not to see the problem. That is a moment in analysis when the therapist must be careful and patient, for a complete reorganization of the *personal* psyche becomes necessary. Dorn, who naturally had the same problems we have, argues about this.

He then continues:

> In all natural things [by which he means chemical materials] there is a certain truth which one cannot see with one's outer eyes but only with the *mens.* This is an experience of the philosophers, and they experienced at the same time that there exists a *virtus* which can produce miracles. Therefore, one should not be astonished that people who have great faith can perform miracles and that they can even submit inorganic matter to their *virtus.*

This idea here has a long history. It entered the Western world through the philosophy of Avicenna, or Ibn Sina, the great Arab theologian and mystic. Like most Islamic sages, he believed in the possibility of performing miracles by magic. He believed in all such things as geomancy, astrology, pyromancy, and so on. We know that Dorn also believed in all sorts of magical proceedings that, having come from late antiquity, lived on in the Arabic world and returned to the Western scientific world in the tenth, eleventh, and twelfth centuries.

In his book about the soul, which was partly translated into Latin in the eleventh century, Avicenna gave the following explanation of magic: namely, that God is self-evidently capable of performing miracles *contra naturam.* He can stop or light a fire, or cure an incurable disease, or do anything else. For Islamic people that is self-evident. Allah is all-mighty. But according to Avicenna's theory, if a magically gifted personality in a state of meditation and inner exaltation can approach this magical creative capacity of the Godhead, then he shares it, so to speak, with God; and if in that stage he violently desires something, it appears in outer nature as a miracle. This teaching was taken over by Albert the Great and then promulgated in the whole Western natural philosophy.

Obviously this refers to what we would call synchronistic events. We too have experienced that whenever an archetype is intensely constellated in someone's unconscious, then outer synchronistic events fitting into the inner situation can happen. We would call this, as Avicenna does, ecstatic contact with the creative power of the Godhead; but synchronistic events happen not only to people in such a state. As Jung points out in his essay on synchronicity, such phenomena generally occur where there is great emotional tension, due to the constellation of an archetype, which always creates a numinous effect.

Whenever an archetype is constellated in someone's psychic material, there is a very great amount of conscious, and sometimes unconscious, emotion, which is observable to the onlooker. In such situations the most frequent clustering of synchronistic events occurs just in the surroundings and at the moment of the outbreak of a psychotic episode, which means that some unconscious archetypal contact is constellated to the bursting point so that the ego complex explodes.

My first experience of this impressed me deeply several decades ago. I was lecturing in a little town in a foreign country, and after my lecture I got absolutely sucked in and eaten up by a man who was obviously schizophrenic, though he was also a very intelligent, gifted artist. I discussed all sorts of topics with him. Then I did not hear anything more about him except for some crazy letters that I never answered, but about half a year later I got a telegram: "Please, please help me, I am double," and his name. As that was during my student years, I had the time, and as there was such desperate pleading in his telegram and the town he lived in was not very far away, I took a train there. When I went to his flat I discovered that he was in the local institution, so I went there.

He was very pleased to see me and was on the way to

recovery. We had quite a nice talk. He told me a most amazing thing, and I checked it with his wife, who confirmed it. He had had a religious Messiah megalomania and was convinced that he would save the world, and that increased slowly. That was the constellated archetype. He became more and more identified with being the new Christ of his age, but finally he got so annoyed with his wife, who did not want to believe that he was Christ, that he took an ax and told her that a devil was sitting in her brain which he could only exorcise by hitting her with the ax and splitting open her head. Quite rightly, she called a doctor, and the doctor called the police. So a doctor with two policemen came to the flat to prevent him from splitting his wife's head open. There was a passage through which one entered into the flat, and at the moment when the two policemen and the doctor went in, the man was standing raving mad in the passage and said, "Now I am the crucified Christ." At that moment there was a great noise. An enormous lamp, a glass luster which they had and which lit up practically the whole flat, burst, and they all stood in the dark among thousands of splinters and groped around till they could take the man to the hospital.

Now, that was a synchronistic event. This man felt, even later, in the hospital where he told me the story, that it was a proof that he was Christ, because when Christ was crucified the light of the sun and the moon darkened! The light went out when Christ was caught by the evil powers! On the other hand, you could just as well understand it not the light of the sun but as a man-made lamp, which would be not the cosmic light but the ego light. The crashing of the light was a synchronistic, symbolic accompaniment of the explosion of his ego, the lamp representing his ego consciousness. But the man interpreted it, which is typical for madness, in the context of his madness.

It is a tragic thing which one very often sees at this stage and which I later also saw in the outburst of psychotic episodes, namely, that these synchronistic events confirm the mad in their madness, because to them it naively seems to be a proof that they are right. Even the outer world begins to behave according to the archetypal myth in which they are swallowed up. So, interpreting the event in the archetypal context with which they are identified, they experience it as a confirmation, which acts as a tragic reinforcement of the destruction of ego consciousness.

This is only one example showing that a kind of emotional ecstasy—or rather, an emotional possession through an archetype—goes together with a greater frequency of events of a synchronistic nature. This also occurs frequently when people are emotionally gripped by some creative process, which is always close to the state of madness; it is just the "positive" version of madness, around which synchronistic events are often clustered.

There are other circumstances when synchronistic phenomena happen. Sometimes they confirm dreams as if to encourage the development suggested by the unconscious. Also, the further one advances, the more one is able to "read" synchronicities. Such situations have naturally already been observed in the past. But back then, they were interpreted not as we do now, as synchronicity, but as magic. In the Middle Ages, for instance, my example would have been interpreted as this man having approached the creativity of God and therefore now sharing God's capacity of being able to explode lamps. Because of the split in the God-image in Christianity, the other party in the Middle Ages would have said that it happened because he had got close to the devil. In other words, where we would have to decide whether to call it a pathological occurrence or a synchronistic event around a creative process, in those times it would have been said to be God in each case, either the God above, or the God below, the Christian God or the Devil: if the synchronicities did coincide with the general weltanschauung, then they were God's work, and if they did not fit, then they were the devil's work. Today we look at this split in other terms, either pathological or nonpathological, but it is the same split. By refusing to accept such categories and taking the experience on a symbolic level, we can help the person to integrate it and thus prevent or shorten the psychotic event.

Many medieval theories about the activities of Christian healers and saints and their ability to perform miracles were explained theologically by Avicenna's theory. Dorn still had that same idea, yet only in the sense of Christian saints; he never bothered much about the problem of the devil, but rather ignored it. In his optimistic Christian outlook he thought that through *virtus*, the alchemist too could get in touch with the creative potential of the Godhead and perform miracles, something many alchemists believed. They discovered more and more that their purely chemical natural scientific endeavors did not help them to make gold, and so they resorted to the idea that it could be achieved by a miracle.

Saint Thomas Aquinas's remark that alchemy does not belong among the natural sciences, that it is a supernatural work like performing miracles, again takes up this idea, which can be found in many other medieval traditions. It is interesting, however, that Dorn believes that the miracle depends not only on contacting the creativity of the Godhead but also on the fact that the same truth as exists in God is also in things. A glass, for instance, in spite of its outer breakable material and its other qualities, would in its essence have something of the creative potential of the Divinity and share in a divine mystery that one cannot see. Outwardly, it is just an ordinary glass, but if you see it with your mental eyes, you can establish the magical contact with it that could make it fly to the ceiling or perform some other miraculous act. You do this by seeing mentally into the essence hidden behind matter.

Dorn continues:

> The body is a prison through which the *virtus* [meaning the magical efficiency of the soul] is blocked and through which the spirit of natural things [i.e., the spirit which would be in this glass] cannot manifest. The spirit in things is something parallel to the religious faith of a human being. People believe that if one dries a

dead poisonous snake and puts it on a wound, it will
magnetically attract the poison. Many people use poisonous snakes to extract the poison from the body, but
they do not ask *why*, they have no theory about it; they
just know that it helps and so do it; but the alchemist
asks why that happens.

According to Dorn, the soul is hampered by the body in
the same way as the spirit of matter is hampered by matter. If
we free both together, then they meet and miracles can be
performed. Dorn does not deny that one can cure an infected
wound by applying the pulverized poisonous snake on it, but
he adds that this proves one can always cure by similarity.
The extract of a pulverized poisonous snake was part of the
medicine of his time. Extracts of venom and of snakes are also
used in medicine today. Dorn thinks that the poison-spirit of
the snake acts on the poison-spirit in the body because like
always attracts like. That was the idea in the medical profession in the sixteenth century, with quite a bit of truth in it.
From this idea they deduced that that factor in the innermost
personality of man, which is his faith or relationship to God,
also exists as a spiritual mystery in things. If those two can
get in touch and be freed, then they synchronize.
Dorn goes on:

The alchemist always investigates in order to discover
from which part of heaven something comes, and then
he investigates the anatomy of the great creature so as
to compare it with the small, the microcosm. This can
be done with four instruments: geomancy for earthly
problems; hydromancy for problems that have to do
with water; pyromancy for problems that have to do
with fire; and astronomy for what has to do with the
heavenly virtues, in the double sense of the word.

Now, here is this strange and interesting idea that the religious faith within the unknown part of a personality coincides

with a spirit in material things, and if they are both freed, miracles can be performed. To investigate that further, one has to use four divination techniques, because one always investigates the anatomy of the macrocosm in comparison with the microcosm.[43]

Here in a very short sketch is the whole philosophy of the Middle Ages, about which you can discover much if you reread Jung's essay on synchronicity. He has several chapters on the technique through which the archetypal concept of synchronicity was previously perceived.[44] What Jung decided to term synchronicity (thus freeing it from this blurred idea of a magical causality) was conceived of in the past (before it was completely discarded at the end of the seventeenth century) as a correspondence: the teaching of the *correspondentia* of microcosm and macrocosm. That, in a way, is the archaic basis of all the magical performances of humankind. For instance, everything has its analogy, and an analogy is not only what we would now call a parallelism of form, but it also has a secret link of effectiveness. For instance, in African rain magic, the most common way of making rain is to pour out a calabash of water while certain incantations and prayers are said, accompanied by certain dances.

In other words, the greater part of all magical activities is the repetition on a small scale of something that at the same time happens on the large, cosmic scale. If this is done with the right psychological attitude, then there is a parallel between what the microcosm (man) does and what happens in the macrocosm (the whole surrounding universe). Rain and fertility charms and all such things are always based on this idea. One of the most frequent beliefs among primitive populations is that the copulation of a husband and wife on the field brings fertility, for what man does is imitated by nature, but here the couple imitates nature and thus encourages her in what she wanted to do anyhow. In the magical idea, in this "primitive" concept of the world, there is such a oneness of inner and outer world and of man and the surrounding universe that they have a natural mutual magical effect upon each other, and I can start at either end. That was an idea that still existed in the sixteenth century.

As already mentioned, when the astrologers saw that somebody had a negative horoscope, they would make chemical countermagic to break the macrocosmic constellation. Giordano Bruno, for instance, had the idea that astrology and the astrological constellations affect the things on earth, and vice versa. Therefore, if one made the right constellations of substances or drawings on an astrological constellation on paper, that would also affect the stars. It was this same idea that caused Pope Alexander VI to require counterhoroscopic activity against his bad horoscope constellation: if the macrocosm affects us with its constellation, it must work the other way around also.

Dorn's teacher, Paracelsus, shared this belief with his pupil, but with a slight difference. Paracelsus did not think that astrological constellations directly affected the body, but believed that within man there is a kind of image of the firmament with its stars, and that the outer constellations of the firmament affect this inner firmament. For instance, the position of Venus in the sky affects the position of my inner Venus, which then affects my physical well-being for good or ill. So Paracelsus had an intermediary opinion, namely, the idea of the inner cosmos of firmament and its reconstellation. This is an interesting beginning of "taking back the projection." We would now say, from a psychological standpoint, that in astrology the contents of the collective unconscious are projected onto the constellations of the sky and that in the case of Paracelsus these projections begin to return into the inner psyche.

Paracelsus believed that the ultimate efficiency comes from the constellations of the stars, but that there is such a thing also within man. The projection is thus taken back into man. We would say the human being has a constellation of archetypes within and is affected by it. Generally, when a projection returns to the person, it first falls into two parts, of which one is integrated and the other discarded. In this an-

cient system you just have this stage where the collective unconscious projected onto the stars partly comes back as
something in man, where it has its double, its reflection, and
can be contacted through different techniques of magic. For
instance, Paracelsus actually practiced geomancy to find out
about earthly things.

Jung was interested in geomancy for a while. You take a
pencil and make a number of dots at random, without count-
ing; or, as Jung did it, you simply take a handful of small
gravel stones and throw them. The idea is to get, by pure
chance, a number of units which you then count off by twos,
and at the end you have one or two dots or stones left over.
You repeat this sixteen times (four times four) and so build up
figures. Let's say that the first time there is one point left
over, the second and third time two, and the fourth time there
is one left; that gives a figure called *carcer*, prison. Another
figure is called *puer*, the child, and so on. There are various
possible figures.

These combinations have names, and you first build four
such figures. Then you throw them around in different mathematical permutations; for instance, you take the upper ones
of the first four, and these first four figures are called the
mothers; the next are the daughters. From the daughters you
get nephews, and from the nephews you make a judge, two
witnesses, and a subjudge, and that gives you the final result.
These figures are exactly like an astrological constellation
and have a symbolic meaning. Prison belongs to Saturn and
means melancholy, hospital, illness; it has all the astrological
associations of Saturn. Each figure has a different archetypal
connotation.

With these figures you make an astrological chart, which
is why they were also called earthly astrology, for instead
of taking the upper, heavenly constellations, you make the
constellation yourself with dots or gravel, and then put it into
an astrological chart and read it as though it were one, or
were a horoscope of transits. Then, just as in astrology, you
can look up in books to see what *carcer* in the first or third

house would stand for, and so on. That is the divination technique of geomancy, very much practiced in those times.

With hydromancy one looks into a bowl of water for direct divination. It is a kind of support for inspiration, like crystal gazing or looking at tea leaves or coffee grounds. I do not know exactly how pyromancy was practiced, but it had to do with looking into the fire. There are different possibilities: either you observe the shape of the flames or the glowing embers, or you burn something and then look at the cracks on it. The Chinese used the tortoise shell. The oldest Chinese oracle, older than the *I Ching*, was to heat a tortoise shell in the fire and then read from the cracks. The Eskimos of northern Canada look at the cracks on a bone that they put into the fire.

I know a village in the canton of Uri in Switzerland where the church and the cemetery are on different sides of the little river, and one crosses by a path and a bridge to get to the cemetery. All funeral processions have to go this way, and when the people walk with or behind the coffin over this path, they always look at the cracks on it, and from that can tell who will be the next to die.

Irregular crack patterns are frequently used for bringing up the knowledge of the unconscious. The technique of melting lead is the same thing. To my mind, these things have to do with a catalyzing effect. I do not believe that the cracks actually do foretell anything, but our unconscious knows. For instance, in that group of people, their unconscious knows through its "absolute knowledge" who is going to die next, but they cannot bring it up directly. They have to look at the confused patterns of cracks, which catalyze the projection.

I came to this conclusion after I once visited a very famous chiromancer who read palms. The lines of the hand always have an irregular pattern and wrinkles. This man put up a very good performance and did it all very scientifically. You had to put your hands on some wax and press to get an imprint. He wrote a book about his method, which seemed very scientific, but I couldn't really "smell" it. So when he finished, I drill-bored into him and asked whether the information was really in the lines. To my amazement he said, "No, it isn't at all!" (though he had written a book about it!). He said, "When someone comes into the room, I know all about that person. [He was a very mediumistic, psychic type of person.] I just know it, but I cannot bring it up, I cannot formulate it: so I use these hand lines. I pretend to look at those lines and then what I know catalyzes or is projected into them. I read from the lines, but actually I know it all when the person came into the room." I think that is why in most primitive divination techniques there is the idea of creating a chaotic pattern into which one can read what one already knows.

In Africa there is a widespread practice: after eating a chicken you take the bones and throw them haphazardly, making a confused pattern, and from the way they fall, you read the situation. It is almost the same thing as when one paints from the unconscious, and it is also the technique of the Rorschach test. You show a lot of dots and irregular patterns to people, and in that way they read what is in the unconscious. The same goes for all the tests having to do with projection. I have read that the Azandes of Sudan give poison to chickens to determine if someone is a criminal.[45] If the chicken dies, the man is guilty; if it lives, he is innocent.

The Azandes repeat the oracle several times to confirm the sentence. That would belong in the same category as walking through fire and other "judgments of God." It is not a question of divination in our sense, it is a question of guilt or innocence, of either/or. I therefore think I would not compare it to these divination techniques, which are playful.

I can explain my idea by the following: In the appendix to Portmann's book on the animal as a social being, he discusses a very puzzling fact concerning the learning capacity of rats. The laboratory rats had to crawl through various kinds of mazes to find their food. The experimenter was certain that the rats could learn; he found that they performed the task 100 percent, so he published the factual results of his experiments. But another investigator, who did not believe that the rats could learn, gave the same kind of maze to the same rats, and they could not do the task but behaved completely stupidly.[46]

A current and widely discussed problem in zoological circles is whether suggestion between experimenters and their subject plays a part. If it turns out to be true that unconscious expectations have an effect on the behavior of animals, how can one make objective experiments? Portmann did not take a stand; he simply published both results. Should it be true that animals can be affected, and I believe it may be true, then just imagine a whole village, in archetypal emotional excitement, squatting around a half-poisoned hen to find out whether John or Jack should be killed! That would constellate a tremendous emotional collective tension and could affect the animal's behavior, if even the belief of just a single investigator can make rats—and not even poisoned rats—more intelligent or more stupid.

In Los Angeles the practice of testing children in order to detect mentally retarded or mentally gifted pupils was abandoned because of research showing that teachers closely identify with the children in their classes. For example, if the teacher was convinced that the children were poor learners, then they would produce low test scores, and vice versa. I think a lot more of those tests and experiments will have to be abandoned, because they are in no way objective. The emotional belief of the experimenter plays an enormous role and influences the potential of a child positively or negatively. When Jung started studying astrology for his book on synchronicity, he believed that the horoscopes for a number of married couples would demonstrate a higher degree of compatibility than a random sample of unmarried people, and they did, to an absolutely amazing extent. But then he felt uneasy and wondered if this was really objective. While sitting in Bollingen, he looked at the stones of his tower—they are irregularly honed—and as the sunlight shone through the leaves, he suddenly saw a face laughing at him from a stone.

(Later he took a chisel and chiseled it out; you can still see it.) Then he felt even more uneasy and thought that the trickster god, Mercurius, had pulled a fast one on him in spite of his marvelous statistical proof![47] He tried to repeat the experiment, this time without any personal conviction, and the statistics played the other way around! So even statistics can play tricks. He published the whole thing in his essay on synchronicity. But though people read it, they do not understand what it means.

I once lectured at the CERN, the nuclear center in Geneva. When I mentioned synchronicity, there were roars of laughter, and these famous physicists said, "Oh, we know that very, very well: our computer absolutely always answers as we expect it to answer. If we believe in a false theory and we are passionately involved, the computer just performs according to what we expect; and then a colleague who does not believe it uses the computer for a few hours and gets a completely different result." This created great amusement. But when I tried to pin them down and say, "Well, gentlemen, then please take that experience seriously," one of them said, "Oh, that's all nonsense, synchronicity is all nonsense." He was in an affect—his tone of voice gave him away.

These physicists admitted the experience but would not take it seriously scientifically, because it would have turned their whole weltanschauung upside down. In spite of their experiences they did not want to admit the truth. It was quite grotesque, for first they laughed and said they knew that the computer did that, and then they pretended that it was nonsense.

This is another example of compartmental psychology. All these mantic procedures are based on the idea of synchronicity or its forerunner, magical causality. Dorn believed in that, and that was what he really ultimately understood by *virtus*, or virtue: the possibility that the human psyche that has become conscious might perform miracles.

# 6

### ❈

# VIR UNUS / UNUS
# MUNDUS

IN THE PRECEDING CHAPTER I cited a passage where
Dorn speaks of the possibility of a more theoretical survey
and insight into the whole situation. He makes a distinction
between doctors and alchemists who use the skeleton of poisonous snakes to extract poison from the blood in a wound,
for instance, but do not think about it, while others, like himself, study the anatomy of the microcosm and macrocosm. Regarding the acquisition of such information, Dorn mentions
four types of divination related to the four elements. Such arts
offer the possibility of understanding the wider connections
of things.

Dorn continues:

> One must therefore always begin with oneself with the
> exercise of frequency. Therefore the *mens* must learn to
> have charity towards his own body and restrict its
> wrong impulses [Now you see the regression: it is the
> body again which is wrong. Dorn had started to with-
> draw the projection, but as soon as the problem of evil
> appeared, he began to shift.] The *mens* must restrict the
> body's wrong desires so that it may serve the *mens* in
> everything, and then it must drink with the *mens* from
> the well of virtue. Then Mens and Body will become one

and will have peace in union. Therefore come, Body, to this well, so that you may drink from it together with the *mens* and after that have no more thirst. O marvelous effect of this well, which makes from two one and makes peace between enemies. The well of love succeeded in making the one *mens* from *spiritus* and *anima*, but this well can also make the one man from the *mens* and the body.

After the second union comes a prayer of thanks that one man, or the inner man, has been produced by drinking together from the well of love. It is quite amazing! The *spiritus* and the soul together made the *mens*, and then came the big split and conflict with the *corpus*. You remember how difficult it was to get those two together and how long they battled, and now, in one quick switch, they are shown drinking together from the well of love and have become one.

The whole product is now called the *vir unus*, which is Latin for the "one man." This refers to ecclesiastical tradition according to which man (as the Church Father Origenes said) consisted originally of many different *mores*—you could say of single characteristic impulses; nowadays we would say of different inherited traits—and, as Origenes also said, until the sinner (the unconscious man) has undergone a Christian conversion and an ethical training in Christianity, he consists of different *mores*.

He said that herds of cattle and flocks of birds, all of different nations, are within you, all pulling in different directions, and only through the grace of the Holy Ghost and by becoming a Christian do you become a *vir unus*, one man—or, as we would now say, a unified personality.

So there you see that what we now call the process of individuation, which has the goal of oneness, becoming one person, was already aimed at in a projected form. Although Dorn did not see all these many cattle and nations within man, he saw that man also consists of different impulses and tendencies and that these must first be separated and clarified and then put together again by the water of the well of love. He then recapitulates the fifth degree: "Each object has its virtue." We know now what virtue means. *Virtus* is not ethical virtue only, but at the same time it means effectiveness. Every object has a certain kind of effect.

> Each object has its virtue and its heavenly influence, which one cannot see with the outer eye, but of which one can only see the effect, as, for instance, the attraction of iron by a magnet. But virtue, the magnetic *virtus*, remains hidden, and one cannot see it in the magnet because it is a spirit.

That is a typically primitive standpoint. It is really a continuation of what one finds in ancient philosophy. Naturally, people were formerly—and primitive people today still are—tremendously fascinated by the effect of magnetism. Like electricity, it was a great mystery to them. One can understand that quite well if one looks at things naively. A magnet, which attracts a bit of iron, has a kind of spiritual effect upon it. To the primitive mind it is a demonstration that spirit can influence matter, and the primitive thinks that this happens all the time and everywhere; in other words, all objects have such electromagnetic powers and thereby exert an influence on surrounding objects. That was what Dorn and the alchemists called the spirit in matter.

> Similarly, wine also has such invisible forces, because its spirit warms and dries one while its body makes one feel cool and moist.

That is very true, for it one drinks wine one is mentally or psychologically warmed up, spiritually and mentally exhilarated; with a wine of good quality one gets into a kind of exaltation, but the body gets heavy and nauseated after an excess of alcohol. For Dorn, the psychological effect of alcohol was another demonstration that material things have what we would call a virtue.

> There are such virtues in other objects also; even bread has its own virtue, and do we not know that the purer parts of bread and wine can be transformed into flesh and blood? [There he makes an amazing jump to the Transubstantiation in the Mass!⁴⁸] Do we not know that from an invisible vegetable form a visible animal form can come!—but naturally it is not the species [that means the outer aspects of bread and wine] which are transformed in that moment, but only the *forma*, in the sense of the Aristotelian and Catholic doctrine. Therefore who could doubt that our art [alchemy] can make much better philosophical transmutations in man than nature could make through bread and wine, and that there are yet other things in nature which have an even greater natural virtue and heavenly influence than the one which you see in bread and wine.

Here, not too clearly (but obviously, if one reads carefully), Dorn alludes to the mystery of Transubstantiation in the Mass, and takes that act as proof for the possibility of a supernatural transformation of coarse material objects. If, through the words of the priest, the bread and wine are transformed into the body and blood of Christ, why should not such possibilities exist everywhere else in nature?

That was a frequent reflection of medieval alchemists. They quite rightly realized that the Transubstantiation mystery of the Mass is in a way an alchemical operation, because the official dogma recognizes that coarse, profane matter, such as bread and wine, suddenly becomes the carrier of the divine reality of the Son of God. He is incarnated in bread and wine. Very many alchemists pounced on this fact and said, "Why should this transmutation be confined only to that little bit of the Host, and that little bit of wine which has been stored in the Church? Why should that not be possible with other substances? If it is possible in principle, it must be possible elsewhere too." This rather shocking expansion of thought was made by many, and you probably remember that in *Psychology and Alchemy*, Jung even quotes an alchemical text written by a Hungarian priest who, step by step, compares the alchemical *opus* with the mystery of the Transubstantiation in the Mass.[49] Dorn here alludes to the same fact:

> He who does not want to believe this must simply first try out the alchemical art; if he does not know that, then he will never learn anything.

Next comes the dialogue between Potentia and the "one man." Mens and the other figures do not exist anymore. Only the *vir unus*, the one man, remains. It is the sixth degree of the opus.

VIR UNUS: Open, please, Potentia.

POTENTIA: Who wants to come in?

VIR UNUS: I have been sent by Virtue.

POTENTIA: Why?

VIR UNUS: To reinforce the virtues which I got from the servant of truth, Frequentia.

POTENTIA: How do you imagine this could take place?

VIR UNUS: Through Potentia.

POTENTIA: Who is Potentia?

VIR UNUS: The *potentia* of truth.

POTENTIA: Where do you think truth lies?

VIR UNUS: I think that truth lies in the truth of God.

POTENTIA: You are worthy of my confirmation. [*Potentia* means a kind of solidification and confirmation—we would call it an increase in the power of the personality.] Therefore

now listen: Potentia, or power, is the constancy of virtue
which one has received from God. Nobody should think that
he could have even the slightest spark of virtue unless he had
been given it by God. Only those who build on the rock of
truth have a stable kingdom. Therefore now be concerned
only with virtue, which is truth itself, so that you become
strong in battle like a lion and that you can overcome all
powers of the world, and so that you do not fear even death
and diabolical tyranny.

I want to get to some more important parts, so I shall go
to the seventh degree, the degree of miracle or philosophy.

> The miracle is the effect of the constancy of truth, and
> to explain this I shall use an example. Once a philoso-
> pher was condemned by a tyrant because he spoke too
> much truth, so the tyrant condemned him to be put alive
> into a hole in a rock and then be slowly squashed with
> iron instruments. But the philosopher cried out: "Well,
> beat me, tyrant, destroy my body, but you cannot de-
> stroy my spirit!" The tyrant got so angry that he or-
> dered the philosopher's tongue to be cut out. But the
> philosopher bit off his own tongue and spat it in the face
> of the tyrant. O look at the marvelous constancy of a
> man who, even when undergoing such martyrdom, took
> death upon himself with pleasure and overcame the tyr-
> anny of the world.

Here in the seventh degree, Dorn, as far as the problems of
evil in the world are concerned, regresses, or has no better
solution than Christianity has offered for the last eighteen
hundred years, namely martyrdom. In spite of his positive
efforts, man will not and cannot change the problems of evil
in the world, but it is a merit to succumb to it in the battle for
good, and that is the true imitation of Christ, who Himself
died as a martyr of evil.

In spite of all his attempts to conceive of a more central
position between good and evil and to integrate the body and

matter, to compensate to a certain extent the one-sided spiritual attitude of Christianity, Dorn gets nowhere in the ultimate ethical realm, but stays within the traditional concepts. In other words, he cannot deal differently with the problem of evil. Then, without further explanation, he recapitulates the seventh degree and makes a conclusion of the whole work.

> The seven degrees of philosophy are also the seven chemical operations by which the artifex can get to the mystery of the marvelous medicine. The philosopher's work is to be compared to the chemical *putrefactio*, because it predisposes one to receive the truth, which is the same as the preparation of natural things for the solution.

Now he goes back to what we had several times before, namely, the lack of one single language by which Dorn could unify physical, chemical facts with psychological facts, he simply begins to make analogies: like this, like that, like this, like that—that's the closest he can come to the union.

> Therefore, while the alchemist studies philosophy [reads alchemical books, for instance], the same thing happens to him as to the metals in the retort, which are first evaporated, dissolved, and prepared for complete liquefication.

Here he uses a word with a double meaning. *Solution* applies to the liquid, the liquefying of metals or other substances in the retort, but it is also the solution of a philosophical or human problem. It is most amusing to see how many terms we still use in psychology that come from this alchemical language of the past. Freud previously spoke of sublimation, we speak of a psychic constellation, and current language uses terms like *volatile* or the "solution" of a problem, and so on. We just do not realize the background of those words, which

have a historical past and originally had a kind of half-chemi-
cal, half-psychological connotation.

> The solution can be compared to philosophical insight:
> just as through the solution one dissolves the bodies [he
> means in the retort], so the doubts of the philosopher
> are dissolved through his insight. Then follows philo-
> sophical love, which creates the frequency of study
> which corresponds to the congelations of the alchemists,
> or the first union in the retort [that means the first so-
> lidification of things in the retort]. And as through fre-
> quent exercise the mind of the philosopher is sharpened,
> so through repeated alchemical washings the different
> parts of the chemical body are made subtle; just as
> through virtue the philosopher becomes one personality,
> so also in the composition the different chemical bodies
> are put together in their smallest parts; also, just as *po-
> tentia* solidifies the personality in its philosophical vir-
> tues, so the *fixatio* of the volatile parts in the chemical
> body solidifies the philosopher's stone, so that the dif-
> ferent vapors cannot evaporate anymore. Just as
> through these philosophical exercises one acquires a
> power which can even perform miracles, so the alchemi-
> cal medicines show their power through projection in
> their perfection.

From the alchemical point of view, projection means that
when you have made the elixir or the *lapis philosophorum*, you
throw it onto other objects, which are thereby "perfected," or
are also turned into gold.

> Now, reader, I have told you the whole intention of our
> work, but you will only achieve something if you pro-
> ceed simultaneously in the true metaphysical philosophy
> just as much as in the natural chemical philosophy. And
> do not complain that it is difficult, because the other
> alchemical authors have blurred this problem very
> much, while I have explained it very clearly. Goodbye,

and whatever, even the smallest good work you can do, take that for advice for yourself.

The opus could end here, but it does not. Dorn adds a sequence of recipes that he calls the philosophical tinctures. *Tincture* means a coloring, any substance that colors another thing.

I could now end my work, but my philosophical love impels me to add also the recipes of the tinctures of my teacher, Paracelsus. I want to explain the secret of what I am going to say, namely, of these different recipes.

Man is created from heaven and earth and from heaven he has his intellect and from earth his body. [*Intellectus* is not the intellect in our modern connotaion. We would have to say consciousness.] From heaven man has consciousness and from the earth the body. What he has from heaven comes from the firmament with even something in it from God which can overcome the powers of the stars. [That means the horoscope.]

If man can transform things outside himself, then he can do that even better within his own microcosm, and he can recognize things even better within himself. Therefore in man himself is the greatest treasure, and nothing is outside him. Therefore one should start from within or from the medium which is outwardly and also inwardly visible, and one must recognize who and what one is within oneself and then one will, within the light of nature, recognize oneself via the outer.

That is one of the most decisive and remarkable parts of the whole text, namely, that man can recognize outer things directly by looking at inner things. Since Dorn's time the West has only tried to recognize directly the outer facts of nature, with a minimum of attention for the subjective factor. It is only during about the last thirty years that in certain scientific circles it has been rediscovered that the mental condition of the observer is a decisive factor in everything we

observe, and that therefore we cannot give an objective de-
scription of outer facts without artificially and self-deceptively
eliminating the subjective factor. The physicist Sir Arthur
Eddington says, in his *Philosophy of Physical Science*, that we
have now ended up realizing that every physical scientific
theory is nothing but a selective subjectivism. By "selective"
he means that one might have certain means of distinguishing
between a nonscientific, speculative, crazy theory and one officially recognized by the team of international physicists.

You see, once it has been accepted that any kind of scientific theory is only a hypothetical construction of the human
mind that will click with outer facts only to a certain extent
and therefore is always historically conditioned, we can be
quite sure that in fifty or sixty years the viewpoint of modern
science will be completely different from what we now believe
to be the ultimate truth. If that were recognized, one could
give up science completely, or say that in that case we are
all justified in making up our own theory, according to our
individual weltanschauung, even about physics, or mathematics, or whatever you like. In those fields, as much as in any
other human field, or in psychology, we can just adopt a theory which suits our own psychological equation.

That would naturally result in completely subjectivistic
chaos. The more responsible scientists, therefore, are trying
to find out what the difference is between a kind of fantastic
subjective theory and a subjective theory of the physicist,
which may be useful and could be applied and repeated and
taught by other scientists. Niels Bohr, for instance, and Wolfgang Pauli formulated the difference by saying that a physical
theory which can be communicated and understood by others
is one which should be recognized as relatively objective,
while one which cannot be communicated or taught to others
should be discarded.

Dorn, as a strongly introversion-oriented personality, anticipates something like that, and says that if a person is not
mentally blind he must first recognize within himself who and
what he is, that is, become conscious of the subjective factors

and of his own subjective motivation in his scientific activity; then, in the light of nature, he will recognize himself via the outer. That means that one can recognize oneself by looking within, or by concentrating on the light of nature within oneself and then looking at what happens to one outwardly.

Now, that is exactly what we do. Jung's idea of self-knowledge does not mean that we subjectively muse about our ego; "I am like that and like that." That may be useful, but it is not what we understand by self-knowledge, which would mean taking the information we get from dreams. In other words, if somebody wants to know himself, in our sense of the word, he has to accept the image which the dream gives about him. If you dream that you behave like a fool, though you subjectively feel most reasonable, you have to take into serious consideration, for, according to the unconscious, or according to the light shed by the archetype of the Self upon your conscious behavior, you are acting like a fool. That is an objective piece of information obtained from a dream whether you like it or not, and you know how often one does not like what one dreams. That is information which comes from the objective psyche within and which we think useful and advisable to accept. That is also what Dorn obviously means by the light of nature.

I cannot go into the history of the concept of the *lumen naturae*, the light of nature, but Jung studied it in "Paracelsica."[50] Viewed historically, the light of nature means what we would now call a kind of consciousness within the unconscious, or simply the intelligence of a dream. If you have analyzed many dreams, you cannot close your eyes to the fact that there is in them an absolutely brilliant intelligence. I am sure we have all often said; "I could have thought about these things for twenty years and not understood them, and now in a dream, the whole thing is clear." If one understands a dream, one has generally this kind of exuberant "Aha!" reaction. That is a light which comes from the "intelligence" of a dream, which naturally one first has to extract through certain methods of interpretation. In the light of dreams one can therefore recognize oneself differently from the ego's opinion about oneself, for it gives additional information which does not come from one's own ego.

A dream is like an objective psychic event, for some light of nature mates with one's ego consciousness and becomes one with it so that both change, and if one is involved in that process, one can also recognize oneself via the outer. That would mean that, if you look at your life in a symbolic way and at the synchronistic events that happen outside, then you will see—if you have a kind of unitarian viewpoint and can transpose your consciousness into the light of nature—that you can even take many outer events as being in the same class of events as dream revelations. At the end of one's life, one could therefore make a complete survey of his or her self-knowledge and of what he or she is by adding up visions and dreams and actual biography and what has happened to him or her. Then an amazing synchronistic connection can be seen between the two, for the actual biographical events of a life have a strange symbolic unity with the inner events. Therefore, if you listen to the biography of, say, an older analysand, and half close your eyes, listening as if it were a symbolic tale, you would have the whole information of the inner life.[51] That is a banal truth and explains why so many books are always written on the connection between character and fate, for the fate of a human being is in a strange way very often linked up with the psychological makeup, which accounts for the saying that every man is his own fate, or carries his own fate in his soul.

This is a very common truth that has always been intuitively perceived. If one looks from within at the things that happen acausally to a human being, or if one looks at them with the *lumen naturae*—that is, with a conscious attitude which is willing to look at the natural patterns within and without—then one can even recognize oneself via what happens outside. One can take that as a part of one's own objective psychological reality.

That was what Dorn was striving at, in a groping way,

and it was something very typical in that he was a physician and therefore naturally saw very deeply into many, many human fates, more than most people in other professions. When a patient rings up a physician or a general practitioner and says he has broken his leg skiing, the doctor—if he knows the patient's whole family situation—cannot help thinking, "Aha, I knew that would happen soon." Such things do happen, and Dorn naturally experienced this a lot and therefore got this idea that what happens outwardly to the human being is in a strange way connected to the objective events in his unconscious, which he knows through the light of nature.

Dorn then moves on to a short chapter about the salt in the human blood and the sulphur in human nature and how these can either cause health or illness. There he attempts a kind of psychosomatic theory which he clearly tries to link up with what he had said before, by showing that the salt and sulphur in the blood of man are influenced by his psychological attitude; the whole balance of health also depends on psychological factors. As you know, salt preserves meat from decaying—it was the method used to preserve meat before the invention of the refrigerator. So Dorn projected the idea that salt in the human blood is the secret which preserved the body from corruption. Then there follows a long polemic on how one always has to watch the salt in human blood and see that it contains the right amount because it has a preserving quality.

He then gives another theory about sulphur in the human body, which he understands as the burning-up effects—in other words, what we would now call oxidization. The oxidization processes in the human body were at that time explained as due to the fact that the body contained a burning sulphur that cooked the contents of the stomach and intestines. All the vaguely expressed cooking processes in the human body were explained by the effect of sulphur. Sulphur was also identified with desirousness and the drivenness of human nature in the negative sense: if you have too much sulphur in your body, then the burning processes in it become too strong and you have to dampen these processes so as to return to the right balance. But sulphur is only negative if it is one-sided and exaggerated; otherwise it is the fiery substance which keeps the whole process going on inside.

This gives us an insight into how Dorn and his contemporaries saw the union of what we now would call the psychic and the somatic factors, namely, through these substances, salt and sulphur, which to him always had a psychological and a physical aspect. For instance, salt has the aspect of Eros, of a sense of humor, or wit and witty detachment, and of wisdom. Sulphur gives the warmth of life, vitality, capacity for participating in life, for having creative fantasies, initiative, and *élan vital*; negatively, it produces one-sided effects with desires and avidity. These substances (which for him are psychosomatic substances) have to be managed correctly and be in the right balance in the body. I cannot go into explaining what one would call a theory of psychosomatic chemistry.

I want to go on with one of Dorn's recipes for producing the quintessence, which you can find in *Mysterium Coniunctionis*.[52] With that historical background information you will be able to see much more what Jung is driving at there.

At the end Dorn gives some recipes for producing the *aqua vitae* (water of life) or Mercurius (Mercury: the vital energy). He says: "The mixture of the new heaven, of honey, Chelidonia, rosemary flowers, Mercurialis, of the red lily and human blood, with the heaven of the red or white wine or of Tartarus, can be undertaken."[53]

Honey symbolizes, in Paracelsus' words, "the sweetness of the earth." It has to do with the pleasure of the senses (also the fear of worldly entanglement). Mercurialis is a plant (dog's Mercury), which, like the Homeric Moly,[54] has magical effects. These are medicinal plants. The red lily stands for the male principle; it is a symbol that produces the *coniunctio*. The white lily symbolizes the inspiration of the Holy Ghost. Chelidonia is a plant that cures eye diseases, heals spiritual melancholy, and protects against outbursts of affect. The red and white wine of Tartarus is a residue also called "body," and is purplish red, which first has to be distilled before it can be added to the mixture.

The result is a "new heaven," the secret truth, or the philosopher's stone. It is identical with the God-image in the human soul. The whole procedure is like an active imagination performed with symbolically meaningful substances, the addition of human blood meaning a complete devotion to the work. (In older times human blood meant the participation of the soul; the signing of pacts with one's blood meant that one put one's whole soul into the matter.) The end result is also described as a four-petaled yellow flower, exactly as in the Chinese text *The Secret of the Golden Flower*. Dorn's recipe runs: Take the inner truth, and your *élan vital* to it, the inspiration of the Holy Ghost, and the capacity to link opposites. Put into this mixture heavenly and earthly love [sex], and then you have an essence with which you can unite heaven and earth. All ingredients are assembled to form the four-petaled yellow flower (i.e., the Self).

With this medicine Dorn also expected to heal people suffering from physical illnesses, whereas we might expect healing to come from, say, chemotherapy or hormones. We know that hormones are strongly linked to emotions and psychic states in general. Fear and stress, for instance, can cause a discharge of adrenaline into the blood. By helping the spirit, one helps the body. In every epoch people believed in chemical substances, on which they projected a psychic meaning. The placebo is a modern example of the effectiveness of the belief that a substance has medicinal properties and that it will work.

Dorn floated over the abysses of the mysteries that Jung was to penetrate. Nevertheless, he was endeavoring to cope with the same problems we cope with, but he could not deal with the problem of evil. After attempting to remove the shadow from the body, he slips and again projects it back into the body. He was caught by and bound to the Christian belief that God is only good and that he cannot contain the problem of evil. Dorn remained a prisoner of the light ethical realm, but in another realm he succeeded in making two unifications.

Summing up, we can see that Dorn has four elements in the inner work of unification and three stages or steps. The four elements are the *spiritus, anima, corpus,* and the *cosmos.* First *spiritus* and *anima* unite and become the *mens.* Then *mens* and *corpus* unite and become the *vir unus,* and finally, in death, the *vir unus* unites with the Universe, though not in its visible form but as the *unus mundus,* its invisible potential background.[55] Before God created the world, He was with His companion, Sophia (Wisdom), or the Word. Sophia is also the soul of Christ, or Christ in His pre-existing divine form before incarnation. According to some medieval philosophers, this Sophia is also the mental image of the creation that existed in God's mind before He created the world. This is associated with the Platonic idea of a metaphysical realm of ideas. In it God conceived the idea of all real things, so that everything on earth has its archetypal model in the *unus mundus.*[56] John Scotus Erigena, for instance, says that all real things existed *in potentia* in God's Wisdom, who is the sum of all archetypes in God's mind. The idea of an *unus mundus* is a variation of our concept of the collective unconscious. First all archetypes are contaminated and thus the *unus mundus* is a unified multiplicity, a separateness of parts and a oneness at the same time. In this imaginary world everything was conceived of as being in harmony. Dorn says that the state of the *unus mundus* only takes place after death; in other words, it is a psychological event by which one becomes one with everything existing.[57]

Concretely, as Jung pointed out, the *unus mundus* manifests in synchronistic phenomena. While we normally live in a dual world of "outer" and "inner" events, in a synchronistic event this duality no longer exists; outer events behave as if they were a part of our psyche, so that everything is contained in the same wholeness.

If the case of the electric chandelier that exploded and crashed to the floor is looked at superficially, it appears that the lamp behaved as if it were a part of what was happening within the man: the extinction of his own light of consciousness.[58] It would be more correct to say that this synchronistic event sprang from a deeper level within the collective unconscious. Psychologically, the man fell into the *unus mundus.*

This experience is the ultimate stage of the process of individuation, a becoming one with the collective unconscious, but not in a pathological way as in certain psychoses where the individuation process has gone astray and everything has been given a wrong twist. When this occurs positively, it brings about a union of consciousness with the collective unconscious instead of an explosion of consciousness; it means an enlargement of consciousness together with a decrease of intensity in the ego complex. When this happens, the ego retires in favor of the collective unconscious and its center, the Self. To reach that point where outer and inner reality become one is the goal of individuation. Through it one also reaches some of what Jung calls the "absolute knowledge" in the unconscious.

In his later years Jung often did not let people talk to him about their problems, but by letting flow what came to his mind he frequently unintentionally told people exactly what they needed. Before one is integrated and individuated, one's own complexes tend to come through. But if one has really worked to solve one's own problems and the complexes are integrated, then one can connect with the collective unconscious and its wisdom can flow through one. At the end point of development (the end stage of the individuation process), the Zen masters are in such a state of harmony with the collective unconscious that they communicate with one another subliminally; they are together in the *unus mundus.*

According to an old Chinese story there were three wise old men who lived separately as hermits in caves. One day they decided to see each other, and two visited the third. They walked in a little bamboo grove and had a delightful time of spiritual communication and oblation. But when they just wanted to cross a little bridge, they suddenly heard a tiger growl, and all three at once burst into laughter! Then they parted. They had understood the synchronicity, for the tiger in China is the female principle of Yin, the fourth in their spiritual male trinity, which they had ignored! So they could "read" events simultaneously, while they were happening, and draw the right conclusions. That is a stage of development man reaches when he approaches death. Perhaps death itself is nothing else than this third stage, the union with the *unus mundus.*

# Notes

1. Juan Vernet, *Die spanisch-arabische Kultur in Orient und Okzident* (Zurich: Artemis Verlag, 1984).

2. H. Jacobsohn, "Das Gespräch eines Lebensmüden mit seinem Ba," in *Zeitlose Dokumente der Seele* (Zurich: Rasher Verlag, 1952). English: *Timeless Documents of the Soul* (Evanston, Ill.: Northwestern University Press, 1968).

3. See C. G. Jung, *Collected Works* (cw), vol. 8, *The Structure and Dynamics of the Psyche*, trans. R. F. C. Hull (Princeton: Princeton University Press, Bollingen Series XX, 1970), chap. 7; cw 13, *Alchemical Studies*, chap. 3.

4. C. G. Jung, cw 13, chap. 2

5. Cf. C. G. Jung, cw 6, *Psychological Types*.

6. E. J. Holmyard, *Alchemy* (Harmondsworth (U.K.) and New York: Penguin, 1957).

7. See Marie-Louise von Franz, *The Golden Ass of Apuleius* (Boston: Shambhala Publications, 1992).

8. Cf. C. G. Jung, cw 12, *Psychology and Alchemy*, chap. 4, part III.

9. See above, note 6.

10. See Marie-Louise von Franz, *Interpretation of Fairy Tales* (Boston: Shambhala Publications, 1996).

11. "The Bath Bâdgerd," in Marie-Louise von Franz, *Individuation in Fairy Tales* (Boston: Shambhala Publications, 1990), pp. 71–149.

12. C. G. Jung, *Memories, Dreams, Reflections* (New York: Vintage Books, 1989).

13. See Barbara Hannah, *Active Imagination* (Boston: Sigo Press, 1981).

14. Jung, cw 12, para. 2.

15. Ibid., p. 25.

16. Ibid., pp. 25f.

17. Ibid.

18. C. G. Jung, cw 13, chap. 3.

19. Lynn Thorndikes's *History of Magic and Experimental Science*, 6 vols. (New York and London: Columbia University Press, 1923), reveals more about his probable sources.

20. Avicenna Latinus, *Liber de Philosophia Prima, sive Scientia Divina* V-X, trans. S. van Riet (Leiden: E. J. Brill, 1980).

21. Cf. Marie-Louise von Franz, *Number and Time* (Evanston, Ill.: Northwestern University Press, 1974).

22. Ibid.

23. "Distractio" does not mean distraction in our sense of the word, though it is implied; it really means a voluntary tearing apart of a well-composed mind from the body so that the body, not the mind, can better search for the truth. The mind already has the truth but the body has the problem.

24. See C. G. Jung, cw 6, *Psychological Types.*

25. See Marie-Louise von Franz, *Shadow and Evil in Fairy Tales* (Boston: Shambhala Publications, 1995).

26. C. G. Jung, cw 11, *Psychology and Religion: East and West*, chap. 6.

27. Corinthians 3:1–2.

28. Adolf Portmann, "Riten der Tiere," in *Eranos-Jahrbuch* (Zurich: Rhein Verlag, 1950).

29. C. G. Jung, cw 14, *Mysterium Coniunctionis*.

30. Ibid.

31. Cf. C. G. Jung, *Memories, Dreams, Reflections*.

32. M.-L. von Franz, *Individuation in Fairy Tales*.

33. M.-L. von Franz, *Shadow and Evil in Fairy Tales*.

34. Wolfgang Pauli, Nobel Prize winner in Physics, 1945. He taught at the Swiss Federal Technical Institute in Zurich, at the same time as Jung.

35. Cf. C. G. Jung, cw 13, chap. 1

36. See J. Marvin Spiegelman and Mokusen Miyuki, *Buddhism and Jungian Psychology: The Ten Oxherding Pictures* (Phoenix, Ariz.: Falcon Press, 1985), pp. 104–13.

37. Cf. C. G. Jung, *Memories, Dreams, Reflections*.

38. M.-L. von Franz, *Shadow and Evil in Fairy Tales*.

39. M.-L. von Franz, *Dreams* (Boston: Shambhala Publications, 1991), "The Dream of Descartes."

40. Cf. C. G. Jung, *Memories, Dreams, Reflections*.

41. C. G. Jung cw 9/ii, *Aion*.

42. M.-L. von Franz, *The Feminine in Fairy Tales* (Boston: Shambhala Publications, 1993).

43. M.-L. von Franz, *Number and Time*, and *On Divination and Synchronicity: The Psychology of Meaningful Chance* (Toronto: Inner City Books, 1980).

44. C. G. Jung, cw 13, chap. 3.

45. A. Evans-Pritchard, *Witchcraft and Sorcery among the Azande of Sudan* (Oxford: Oxford University Press, 1937).

46. Adolf Portmann, "Biologie and das Phänomen des Geistigen," in *Eranos-Jahrbuch* (Zurich: Rhein Verlag, 1946).

47. See C. G. Jung, cw 9/i, *The Archetypes and the Collective Unconscious,* chap. 5.

48. See C. G. Jung, cw 12.

49. Ibid., paras. 480–89.

50. C. G. Jung, cw 13, chap. 3.

51. M.-L. von Franz, *Interpretation of Fairy Tales.*

52. C. G. Jung, cw 14, *Mysterium Coniunctionis,* para. 681.

53. Ibid., para. 683.

54. "Moly," in botany "golden garlic," is a mythical and alchemical plant described in the poems of Homer. In *The Odyssey,* Hermes gives this plant to Ulysses as a protection against Circes' artifices.

55. M.-L. von Franz, *C. G. Jung: His Myth in Our Time* (Boston and Toronto: Little, Brown, 1975), chap. 12.

56. M.-L. von Franz, *Creation Myths* (Boston: Shambhala Publications, 1995), chap. 3

57. Cf. M.-L. von Franz, *C. G. Jung: His Myth in Our Time,* chap. 12.

58. See page 122.